ACCESS YOUR ONLINE RESOURCES

Animal-Assisted Learning contains a number of printable online materials, designed to ensure this resource best supports your professional needs.

Go to https://resourcecentre.routledge.com/speechmark and click on the cover of this book.

Answer the question prompt using your copy of the book to gain access to the online content.

ANIMAL-ASSISTED LEARNING

Animal-Assisted Learning is an essential guide to transforming teaching practices through the integration of animals into educational settings.

The book explores how animals can significantly enhance cognitive, emotional and social development, turning education into an engaging, life-affirming experience. Packed with professional wisdom, chapters:

- Delve into the psychological benefits of animal therapy that support mental health, particularly for children with special educational needs or those in early years settings.
- Cover the practicalities of bringing animals into your environment, from risk assessments to ethical considerations, ensuring a safe and enriching space for all.
- Contain a wealth of real-life case studies illustrating the transformational impact of animal-assisted learning in a range of settings.

Combining a theoretical background with detailed practical guidance, this book offers a new way of doing things. It is an essential, inspiring resource for all early years and primary educators, SEND practitioners, care workers and anyone passionate about making learning inclusive, effective and joyful for every child.

Jenny Phillips currently works as a teacher and has qualifications in Farm and Animal Therapy and an MA in Inclusive Education, specifically focusing on the therapeutic use of animals with children who have SEN to help education, development, growth, health and wellbeing. Jenny has previously worked as a paediatric/neonatal nurse and SEND practitioner, and as a lecturer in Child Health at Middlesex University.

Dawn Newman is a communities engagement and membership professional with a background in project management and employability, and an MSc in Digital Journalism. She previously worked for NCFE, where she was responsible for the systems, strategy and forward direction of CACHE Alumni, a membership organisation for care, health, early years and education.

ANIMAL-ASSISTED LEARNING

An Educator's Guide

Jenny Phillips and Dawn Newman

LONDON AND NEW YORK

Designed cover image: Jenny Phillips and Dawn Newman: Eric, the lovely sheep; Buckly, the rescue rabbit and Walter, the hearing dog

First published 2026
by Routledge
4 Park Square, Milton Park, Abingdon, Oxon OX14 4RN

and by Routledge
605 Third Avenue, New York, NY 10158

Routledge is an imprint of the Taylor & Francis Group, an informa business

© 2026 Jenny Phillips and Dawn Newman

The right of Jenny Phillips and Dawn Newman to be identified as authors of this work has been asserted in accordance with sections 77 and 78 of the Copyright, Designs and Patents Act 1988.

All rights reserved. The purchase of this copyright material confers the right on the purchasing institution to photocopy or download pages which bear the support material icon and a copyright line at the bottom of the page. No other parts of this book may be reprinted or reproduced or utilised in any form or by any electronic, mechanical, or other means, now known or hereafter invented, including photocopying and recording, or in any information storage or retrieval system, without permission in writing from the publishers.

Trademark notice: Product or corporate names may be trademarks or registered trademarks, and are used only for identification and explanation without intent to infringe.

British Library Cataloguing-in-Publication Data
A catalogue record for this book is available from the British Library

ISBN: 978-1-041-09279-7 (hbk)
ISBN: 978-1-041-09276-6 (pbk)
ISBN: 978-1-003-64930-4 (ebk)

DOI: 10.4324/9781003649304

Typeset in Interstate
by Deanta Global Publishing Services, Chennai, India

Access the online resources: https://resourcecentre.routledge.com/speechmark

CONTENTS

About the Authors — xiii
About this Book: How to Use this Guide — xvi

1 The Educational Power of Animals — 1
   The Heart of Animal-Assisted Education — 1
   The Holistic Benefits — 4
   Understanding the Sensory Connection — 4
   Theoretical Foundations — 5
   Emotional and Social Development — 8
   Cognitive and Academic Skills — 9
   Sensory and Physical Benefits — 11
   Behaviour and Wellbeing — 12
   Example Use Cases for Cross-Curricular Integration — 12
      Mathematics — 12
      Science — 12
      Language Arts — 12
      Physical Education — 12

2 Animal Therapy in Action: The Psychological Power of Animals in Education Settings — 15
   Regulating Emotions Through Animal Interactions — 15
      How Animals Help Children Feel Safe, Seen and Ready to Learn — 15
      Regulating Emotions Through Animal Interactions — 17
   Therapeutic Application Focus — 17
      Animal-Assisted Therapy in Action — 17
      Animals in Emotional and Physical Therapy — 21
      The Therapeutic Impact of Fur, Scales and Feathers — 22
      Lessons from Dementia Care Practice — 23
   Substance Dependence Syndrome Treatment — 24
   Skunks and Schizophrenia — 25
   Animal Support in Narrative Therapy — 26
      A Bridge to Connection — 27

viii Contents

3 Introducing Children to Animals and Farm Therapy (A Process)	29
Laying the Groundwork	29
Understanding Your Goals	29
Bringing the Vision to Life	31
Choosing the Right Animals	31
Step by Step	36
Designing Ethical, Effective Animal-Assisted Provision	36
Matching Provision to Children's Needs	37
Start with Why	40
You Don't Have to Do It All at Once	40
Prep and Parents	40
Preparing Children for Animal Companions	42
Creating Safe Spaces for Learning with Animals	42
Building Routines	44
Maintaining the Environment	45
Animal Introductions Checklist	49
Intention and Planning	49
Preparing Children and Staff	50
Environment and Practical Set-Up	51
Routine Building and Integration	52
Whole-School Culture and Celebration	53
Keeping the Theory in Mind	55
Reconnecting to Purpose	55
Holding on to Your North Star	55
Using OKRs to Stay on Track	55
Scope Creep	56
Mission Creep	56
Remember Why You Started	57
4 Risk Assessing Animal Interactions	58
Starting Your Risk Assessment	59
A Chance to Reflect	60
Putting It All Together	62
What Are the Hazards?	62
Adding Controls	63
Reviewing Risk Levels	64
Filling in the Blanks	65
Incorporating Feedback	66
Thinking Through the Risks Checklist	67
Setting Up for Safety Checklist	68
Avoiding Burnout Checklist	69

5	The Boring Stuff: Business Casing, Planning and Overcoming Objections in an Educational Setting	70
	What Is a Business Case?	70
	The Principles of a Business Case	71
	1. Delivering Value Quickly	71
	2. Iterative Learning	71
	3. Learner-Centred Outcomes	71
	4. Flexible Funding	71
	Scoring Your Case – Before You Submit	72
	Rough Business Case Scorecard	72
	How to Use Objections	72
	Building Your Business Case	74
	A. Executive Summary	74
	B. Objectives	74
	C. Benefits	74
	D. Options Considered	76
	E. Costs and Financial Plan	79
	F. Risks and Mitigations	81
	G. Project Plan	81
	H. Conclusion and Call to Action	82
6	Farm School Is Open! Now What?	83
	Riverside Education: A Whole-School Approach to Animal-Assisted Learning	83
	Background	83
	The Challenge	84
	Approach	84
	Integrating Learning with Practicality	85
	Making Real Progress	85
	Challenges	85
	A Whole-School Approach	86
	Results and Impact	86
	Learning Through Practice	87
	Lessons Learned	87
	Emzi Mills-Frater: Building an Animal Education Centre	88
	Background	88
	The Challenge	88
	Approach	89
	Inclusive, Practical Education	89
	Strategic Relationships	90
	Strong, Values-Driven Team Culture	90
	Results and Impact	92
	Lessons Learned	92

Contents

- Lesley Forrester: Northern Animal Assisted Therapies and Activities (NAATA) — 93
  - Background — 94
  - The Challenge — 94
  - Approach — 95
  - Responsive, Child-Led Practice — 95
  - Strategic Practice and Safeguarding — 97
  - Results and Impact — 97
  - Lessons Learned — 98
- Jayne Haigh: Goxhill Meadows Hearts and Minds — 99
  - Background — 99
  - The Challenge — 100
  - Approach — 100
  - Trauma-Informed and Child-Led — 100
  - Relationships First, Paperwork Second (But Not Forgotten) — 101
  - Results and Impact — 102
  - Lessons Learned — 103
- Jenny Phillips: Starting from Scratch — 104
  - Background — 104
  - Approach — 105
  - Child-Led Interaction — 105
  - Sensory Learning — 105
  - Never Assume — 106
  - Lessons Learned — 106
- Ryan Perry: A First-Generation Farmer with a Passion for Rare Breeds and Public Service — 107
  - Background — 107
  - The Challenge — 108
  - Space Costs Money – But So Does a Lack of It — 109
  - Approach — 110
  - Conservation and Education — 110
  - Exploring Opportunities — 111
  - History and Culture — 111
  - Curriculum Links — 111
  - Results and Impact — 112
  - Lessons Learned — 113
- Josh: Noah's ART — 113
  - Background — 113
  - The Challenge — 114
  - Approach — 115
  - Animal-Assisted Therapy, Rooted in Evidence — 116
  - Confidence, Not Compliance — 116
  - Results and Impact — 117
  - Lessons Learned — 117

Evidence-Informed, Person-Centred Support Works	117
The Power of Non-Verbal Communication Shouldn't Be Underestimated	118
Quality Comes from Structure and Care	118
Small Steps Lead to Big Change	118
Cedars School, Gateshead: Animal-Assisted Wellbeing Interventions	119
Background	119
The Challenge	120
Impact	120
Lessons Learned	120
Matthew Colley: A School-Based Pracademic	121
Background	121
The Challenge	121
Approach	122
Focus and Empathy	123
Trauma-Informed Practice	123
Challenges	123
Results and Impact	126
Lessons Learned	126
7 No Room? Don't Worry! Ways to Incorporate Animal Learning Without Animal Care Responsibilities	128
Animal Imagery and Visual Learning	129
Simulations and Role-Playing	131
Virtual Tools and Tech-Based Learning	131
In Focus – Real-Life Examples	132
Postcards from the Hutch – A Preschool Letter-Writing Adventure	132
The Reading Tree – A Storytime Adventure with Animal Friends	133
Animal Celebration Day – A Day of Learning and Laughter	134
Chickens and Creativity – Making Observation Tangible	135
Canines, Coffee and Curriculum – A Tail-Wagging Study Support Event for Paediatric Nursing Students	135
On the Farm – Exploring Animal Therapy in Paediatric Care	136
8 FAQs and Troubleshooting	140
General Questions	140
Best Animals for Different Settings	141
Common Issues and Troubleshooting	142
UK Law and Legal Considerations	142
Key Legislation	142
The Five Welfare Needs (Animal Welfare Act 2006)	143
The Performing Animals (Regulation) Act 1925	143
What Hooks Could Be Used in Lessons or Therapy to Capture Interest?	143
Further Resources (UK)	144

9 Finding (or Inventing) Your Own Career Path with Children and Animals   145
    Matthew Colley   146
        Animals Came First   147
        'I Don't Want to Be a Teacher'   148
    Abide Zenenga   150
        From Research to Riverside   151
    Jenny Phillips   153

Bibliography   *157*
Index   *160*

ABOUT THE AUTHORS

Jenny and Dawn met at an early years conference in 2018 and immediately knew that they wanted to work together. Despite being engaged in very different careers, they found a real shared passion for animals and have embarked on some lovely sharing projects over the years of their friendship so far, to help others to see the amazing value in animal-based provision within care, health, early years and education. This book is the culmination of their learning and passion for animals in education.

Jenny Phillips is a caring and enthusiastic educator whose diverse experience, deep care for children and long-standing commitment to inclusive practice make her an invaluable contributor to any work centred on animal-assisted education. She brings a rare blend of academic credibility, hands-on expertise and ethical clarity. Jenny is uniquely placed to speak to the realities, challenges and rewards of integrating animals into learning environments for some of our most vulnerable learners.

Jenny's career has always been rooted in care. She began working in nursery settings and early years education before moving into paediatric nursing, specialising in neonatal care and later becoming a senior lecturer in child health. Her return to classroom-based work in recent years, most notably as a SENCO and Forest School practitioner, has seen her bring that depth of clinical knowledge and developmental understanding into settings that directly support children with additional needs. This layered insight into health, education and child development gives her a rare 360-degree view of children's experiences and needs.

Her academic background includes not only an MA in Inclusive Education but also higher-level studies in educational leadership and management, alongside a raft of animal-assisted therapy qualifications. She is a certified fellow of the Higher Education Academy and has trained extensively in areas such as care farming, neonatal health, child protection and working with children with SEND. She has even contributed to curriculum development, equipping future professionals with the tools and understanding needed to meet children's complex needs compassionately and effectively.

What makes Jenny stand out, though, is her capacity to bridge sectors in ways that feel both grounded and imaginative. Her experience ranges from running practical sensory-based activities with young children to lecturing in university settings. Whether leading a forest-based group activity or advocating for high-quality safeguarding procedures, Jenny understands how to adapt her approach to meet the needs of both learners and animals. She is methodical, curious and always centred on the needs of those that she supports.

Jenny's involvement in the farm-based and therapeutic education space is a deeply informed, well-researched area of practice. She has completed the CEVAS accreditation for countryside educational visits, engaged with care farming frameworks, and has extensive training in animal-assisted therapy and inclusive provision. She also continues to upskill, and there's never been a year when Jenny hasn't completed a formal qualification of some sort!

As an author and contributor to this book, Jenny offers an evidence-based, values-driven perspective rooted in lived experience. She can speak fluently about the intersection of child development, animal welfare, educational practice and therapeutic intervention. Whether she is sharing anecdotes from the classroom, designing inclusive activity plans or reflecting on the complexities of risk and reward in animal-based provision, she writes and works with warmth, integrity and a clear-eyed commitment to improving children's lives.

You'll learn more about Jenny's practice in this book. You can read the story of Jenny's animal provision in Chapter 6 and find out more about her career in the case study in Chapter 9.

Dawn Newman is a highly experienced community builder and strategic communications professional, with a track record of leading engagement initiatives in education, care and membership-based organisations. Her background includes over nine years at an awarding organisation, where she led the development and growth of a professional membership network for practitioners in the care, health, early years and education sectors, and introduced a range of impactful resources, including a member magazine, employability toolkits and an award-winning podcast. Dawn's focus is on building inclusive professional communities, facilitating learning and applying strategic insight to digital platforms and content ecosystems. Her experience spans membership management, stakeholder engagement, digital journalism and multi-channel content strategy, with particular strengths in creating environments that support lifelong learning and professional development.

In addition to her professional expertise, Dawn is a certified yoga teacher and has qualifications in digital journalism and marketing. Her multidisciplinary background includes roles in careers advice, homelessness services, project management, publishing and education, through which Dawn has spent years shaping the professional journeys of people working to make the world a better place for children and vulnerable groups.

Dawn has hands-on experience with livestock and animal care through her ongoing involvement in community farming. After initially volunteering on a local community farm, she now supports friends with smallholdings and assists with the holiday care and handling of animals such as sheep, goats, poultry and waterfowl. This includes supporting lambing season, feeding routines, basic husbandry and observation of animal behaviour and welfare. Her experience with livestock is not formalised through a commercial operation, but is nonetheless grounded, practical and informed by close collaboration with working farms.

In her own words, Dawn describes herself as a 'Jack of all trades, master of none', and she has worked in various roles across music venues, betting shops, employment support organisations and corporate communications. Dawn is always learning and making connections, and advocates for a 'curiosity-based' approach to career exploration and personal development.

This combination of experience makes Dawn well placed to co-author a book on animal-assisted education. She brings an understanding of how to structure and scale inclusive learning communities, how to communicate complex and sensitive topics, and how to engage diverse professional audiences. Her professional background also gives her insight into the operational and ethical considerations involved in education, safeguarding and service delivery, which are key concerns in the context of using animals in educational settings.

ABOUT THIS BOOK: HOW TO USE THIS GUIDE

We've tried to write this book so that it makes sense in order, and so that you can use it to understand, plan and produce your own animal-assisted project in an education setting. But the truth is, we can't know how you'll use this book – or how you should use it for the best. One of the central messages of this project is that plans rarely survive contact with real-life situations, and because of this, you'll probably find different parts of this book helpful at different times, or in different ways. That's how we've designed it – so that it can be used and read however you see fit.

If you're a vocational learner who likes to figure things out as you go, you are definitely in luck here. Animal provision only works if you can take an agile approach to planning and delivery. Animals don't come with an instruction manual, and they're not always good at taking direction! You'll probably most enjoy the practical elements of this book, where you'll research your animals, plan your delivery and use the chapters as a guide to building your own plan, paying less attention to the theory. Although you might choose to skip the more academic sections of the book, where we talk about the theoretical foundation and the studies that show where animals can add value, they'll become valuable when writing your project's business case, as repositories of quotes and useful information, to help you to demonstrate your case.

If you're a bookworm and enjoy deep research and theory-first practice, you'll also find a home here. The first two chapters of the book set a strong foundation for your work with animals and provide rich fodder for your own research and for diving into learning about why what you're doing works.

Whether you're looking for a checklist to help guide your way or trying to make a case with facts and links to academia, you'll find help in these pages.

There's a mix of stuff here, with some theory at the beginning, to help demonstrate why animals can add value to learning and to the overall wellbeing of learners and colleagues alike. And then, moving on from the theory and the case for 'why', there's support with the 'how' – both from an academic and from a relational perspective, with lesson plans and activity ideas, and with some support to develop your plan and decide the logistics of how best to carry it out. We aim to help you feel confident that you've got all bases covered, while leaving plenty of space for you to build something unique, to serve the unique learners, space and situation that you're looking to support.

On the journey, we'll offer prompts to help you to reflect and embed your learning, and to help you to design a provision that truly works for you.

Don't feel bad about skipping ahead, to the bits that you'll find most interesting, and there's no harm in going back to the bits that you want to read again. Maybe after reading a case study, a concept will become easier to picture, or you might find that working through the checklist prompts questions that make you want to revisit an idea you read earlier. So, although it can be read from the beginning to the end, this book is not linear and there's no real right way to read it. This is a resource. Take from it what you need.

1

The Educational Power of Animals

> Animals in the classroom have the power to transform learning and make it an immersive experience. From teaching biology through observation to instilling mathematical concepts through feeding schedules, weighing and observing, animals offer a dynamic way to engage with core curriculum subjects. This chapter explores how animal interactions can enhance learning through opportunities for cognitive, social and emotional development, while supporting the curriculum with tangible, real-life applications for learning in context.

The Heart of Animal-Assisted Education

You might have heard of school dogs and class rabbits and thought 'that sounds nice', or maybe you've seen examples of holistic education that centres around animal delivery, but there's such a breadth of different kinds of animal-assisted learning that it can be difficult to know what 'counts'. We're not going to do much, in this book, to help you build a rigorous academic understanding of what counts as animal therapy, and what might be better classified as animal-assisted learning, but it's important to know that there is a distinction and that, in many circumstances, it's an important one.

At its core, animal-assisted education is a purposeful approach which can enhance children's learning and development, whether they're interacting with stick insects, dogs, horses or any of the other great options for therapeutic and educational interaction. Embedding animals into educational activities can support practitioners to prepare engaging experiences which, ultimately, have the potential to help students better understand and retain academic concepts.

While animal-assisted education focuses on enhancing learning and development through meaningful animal interactions, animal therapy differs in that it involves structured, goal-led interventions facilitated by trained professionals such as therapists or counsellors. Rooted in evidence-based practice, animal therapy uses the natural, non-judgemental presence of animals to support emotional wellbeing, build trust and help individuals process complex experiences.

DOI: 10.4324/9781003649304-1

2 *Animal-Assisted Learning*

Figure 1.1 Buckly the rabbit receives messages and pictures from the children in his setting as part of their letter writing topic

Where education sessions might focus on academic or social learning, therapy sessions are designed to meet specific therapeutic aims such as managing anxiety, improving communication or supporting trauma recovery.

The introduction of animals can be particularly valuable for learners who may find traditional teaching approaches challenging, or for those who need to see learning in action to understand its applications, but it's possible that all children could benefit from access to animal-assisted education – in fact, there are plenty of benefits for adults too!

Because of the overlap in benefits and the shared values between animal therapy and animal-assisted learning, you'll see us referring to both, sometimes interchangeably, in the pages of this book. Remember – animal therapy is always carried out by trained therapists, but animal-assisted education and other animal interventions can benefit from considering their therapeutic qualities, even in the classroom. For example, interaction with rabbits has been shown to provide tactile stimulation and comfort, often used in play therapy to facilitate emotional expression and reduce anxiety in children. (Fine, 2010, p. 145).

The presence of animals can transform the learning environment and can make it feel much more welcoming and conducive to learning for all students, while animals provide fertile ground for contextualised learning, making lessons easier to adapt for learners of differing ability. You might already be wondering how introducing animals will calm your classroom or imagining the excitement that might follow an announcement about the new class

Figure 1.2 An animal classroom at St Lukes School with tables and natural perches and decoration

Figure 1.3 Animal housing in a classroom at St Lukes

rabbits, but don't worry. We're going to share lots of examples, case studies and advice that will help you to make the transition as smooth as possible.

Every animal introduction will be different, because every child, educator and setting is unique. It's a complex topic and one that you might have been grappling with for a while.

Over the course of this book, we'll lay the foundations for you to build your own bespoke case for animal-assisted education in your setting. Using case studies and examples of animal provision done well, we'll demonstrate a framework for building a case that's backed by scientific reasoning, which takes into account the unique circumstances of individual classroom settings when it comes to health and safety considerations, shows good financial planning and, most importantly, accounts for the needs of the unique children who might attend.

The Holistic Benefits

While many recognise that animals can improve our physical and emotional wellbeing, there's increasing evidence in favour of their potential in supporting learning more directly.

When applied well, animals can help to foster a deep sense of psychological safety, support children to feel calm and supported when in the classroom and can help to encourage understanding that it's OK to get things wrong and to keep trying, developing children's resilience and tenacity.

When children feel safe and supported, they're better positioned to learn. This can help to lay the foundations for a learning environment where both academic and personal growth can be centred around a third entity, reducing pressure, and also for an environment where teaching about self and co-regulation can be 'baked in' to the day-to-day. According to Swansea University, interacting with animals has potential positive benefits for children's social, emotional, physical, behavioural and cognitive development, and it's possible that the benefits of animal-assisted education could be wide-ranging, including:

- Enhanced attention and memory
- Improved motivation to learn
- Better social and communication skills
- Increased emotional awareness and empathy
- Reduced anxiety and stress
- Greater physical engagement in learning

Understanding the Sensory Connection

Animals can provide rich sensory experiences which naturally engage children in learning. Drawing on Laird's sensory theory (1985), we understand that learning is enhanced when multiple senses are engaged. Through sight, sound, touch and even smell, interactions with animals can contribute to memorable learning experiences which can help children to retain information more effectively.

As Aristotle is credited with having noted, 'There is nothing in the intellect that was not first in the senses.'

Humans experience everything through the lens of our senses. Our memories and experiences shape how we understand the world and the concepts which we apply to it.

More recently, Barbara Isaacs explained, 'Sensory experiences boost brain development and lay the foundations for later academic success.' And although Aristotle and Isaacs weren't talking specifically about animal-assisted education, this means that sensory experiences, which animals can help to provide, have the potential to literally and directly impact on our brain development and help us to achieve more.

Animals are already deeply embedded in children's lives; as Patty Born Selly (2014, p. 3) points out, they are 'a central part of every child's landscape', appearing not only as family pets and wild creatures but also in toys, books and media. But we're not quoting these core educational theories because there's not lots of more specific research. In fact, the integration of animals in education actually builds upon a rich history of nature-based learning theories, and recently, the field has expanded to include Animal-Assisted Sensory Education (AASE), which specifically recognises the unique sensory benefits animals bring to learners of all kinds.

Incorporating animals into settings also allows for a sensory-rich environment that can cater to children's natural curiosity. Play with animals can involve different textures, sounds and movements, enhancing sensory integration. In construction play, children might build habitats or toys for animals, learning about engineering, physics and animal needs. Role-play scenarios involving animals can take children from the classroom to imagined pet shops, veterinarian offices or farms, enriching their understanding of community, communication and care.

Exploration play with animals encourages children to investigate the natural world, understanding ecosystems and animal behaviour. Socio-dramatic play, where children enact scenarios with animals, develops communication, teamwork and problem-solving skills. Even fine motor activities like threading beads to make animal toys or puzzles or cleaning out small animal cages, can sharpen dexterity while keeping the connection to nature alive.

Theoretical Foundations

Several prominent educational theorists have advocated for nature-based learning approaches that align with the case for animal-assisted education:

Figure 1.4 Crocheted animals can provide comfort to the recipient and develop dexterity in the maker

- **Rudolph Steiner (1861-1925)** emphasised connecting with the natural world through feeling, doing and thinking. His approach recognised that children are naturally receptive to learning from their environment and benefit from sensory-rich experiences.
- **John Dewey (1859-1952)** believed in learning through real-world experiences and interactions. His philosophy supports the potential for the hands-on, experiential learning which animals naturally facilitate.
- **Jean-Jacques Rousseau (1712-1778)** advocated for learning through direct experience with nature, and believed that it is essential for holistic child development. His emphasis on sensory learning aligns perfectly with the case for animal-assisted education.
- **Maria Montessori (1870-1952)** stressed the importance of connecting children with nature, famously stating that 'The land is where our roots are' and that 'Children must be taught to feel and live in harmony with the earth'. Her sensory approach to learning naturally encompasses animal interactions, and she spoke directly about the potential for animals to assist in creating good educational experiences.

The Educational Power of Animals 7

- **Howard Gardner (1943-)** developed the theory of multiple intelligences, which includes naturalistic intelligence – our innate ability to connect with and understand the natural world. His work helps us understand how animal interactions can support different types of learners.

The natural world, including interaction with animals of all shapes and sizes has played a crucial role in educational theory and practice for generations. It's entirely possible for the animal-assisted education projects of today to build upon this theoretical foundation to offer innovative approaches to learning.

Whether it's a class pet, visiting therapy animals, trips out or a remote solution, there's evidence that regularly working with and alongside animals can help improve focus, communication, emotional regulation and social skills. For example, Vanfleet and Faa-Thompson found that 'rabbits can improve social skills in children with developmental disorders through consistent and gentle handling' (2018, p. 89), highlighting the value of calm, repeated interaction in nurturing connection and confidence.

Figure 1.5 Members of the public learn about sheep at a city farm in Gateshead

8 *Animal-Assisted Learning*

Figure 1.6 Walter the hearing dog joins in with a school reading challenge

Emotional and Social Development

There's real potential for animals to support children with emotional development.

Animals can help to provide a sense of acceptance and an understanding of co-regulation, reducing social anxiety and helping children feel safe. Caring for and interacting safely with an animal can foster empathy, responsibility and patience. And non-verbal children or those with communication barriers might feel more comfortable expressing themselves around animals. As Fine explains, 'the human–animal bond forms the foundation for animal-assisted interventions that support physical, emotional, and social functioning' (2010, p. 8), reinforcing just how far-reaching these benefits can be.

This focus on a 'third entity' can also help to take the pressure off children, allowing them to interact more indirectly with practitioners, educators and therapists working in educational settings.

As Martin and Farnum (2002) observed, 'animals act as transitional objects, allowing children to establish bonds with them and then extend these bonds to humans... animals may be one way to increase attachment between children with PDD [pervasive developmental disorders] and their social environment'. This indirect pathway to connection can be particularly powerful for children who find direct social engagement challenging.

Perhaps most importantly, animals can help to foster emotional intelligence and social skills. Through caring for animals, children can:

- Develop their sense of empathy and their emotional awareness
- Learn to recognise and respond to others' needs and to understand that the reactions of others can be informed by multiple factors
- Build self-esteem through responsible pet care, gaining confidence as they master new skills and develop their sense of accountability.

> The practitioners we spoke to during our interviews for the case studies section of this book all spoke about how animals 'unlocked' something in their practice, one way or another. If you're struggling to imagine what a good animal-assisted education project might look like, there's no harm in heading there first. You can always come back here and re-read them when you get to them, to pick up on any additional context.

Cognitive and Academic Skills

Interacting with animals naturally gives rise to curiosity and inquiry-based learning. Children usually formulate questions about animal behaviour, habitats and care needs relatively quickly, and this natural curiosity can be channelled into meaningful learning experiences across multiple subjects. These curious interactions also provide educators with the opportunity to reply with 'I don't know. What do you think?' to empower children to interpret animal behaviour for themselves and foster an environment of exploration and psychological safety around inquiry. Modelling that it is OK to not always have the answers can contribute to the psychological safety of the setting and allow children to feel safe exploring and finding out as they go, making lessons more hands-on and child- (or animal-) led.

Feeding schedules and weighing animals can help to integrate maths concepts like measurement, time and sequencing, while supporting children's motivation to learn and their ability to understand concepts that might feel unimportant when taught in a more traditional, abstract setting. Less apparently tangible benefits can also be linked back to animal-assisted interventions, like the development of skills in descriptive writing. Children's communication has been shown to improve when they are given the opportunity to talk or write about their own animal experiences.

10 *Animal-Assisted Learning*

Figure 1.7 Chickens try to speed up the feeding process

Figure 1.8 Measuring feed for animals can help learners to develop maths skills

Alongside the more measurable educational benefits, animals can serve as natural catalysts for both verbal and non-verbal communication. Children learn to interpret body language and develop communication skills through animal interactions, which might be particularly valuable for students who struggle to recognise emotions in others (or in themselves). Introducing difficult concepts without them feeling personal can help to create a psychologically safe environment, more conducive to learning, in the same way that animals can allow children to practise verbal communication and storytelling skills without fear of judgement.

Sensory and Physical Benefits

Perhaps the most obvious and tangible benefits of animal interactions are in the sensory benefits. We covered this briefly earlier in this chapter, but with examples in context, it's possible to understand how this sensory engagement might work.

Animal care activities provide excellent opportunities for developing both fine and gross motor skills. Through gentle handling, grooming, feeding and play activities, children naturally engage in purposeful physical movements that enhance their coordination and motor control, as well as providing better motivation than exercise 'for its own sake'.

Stroking fur, feeling different textures and listening to animal sounds engage multiple senses, supporting children who experience difficulties with sensory processing or who may be feeling unsettled. Having a sensory 'anchor' can help us to self-soothe and co-regulate

Figure 1.9 School pets, like Maple, can help to provide a sensory anchor

emotions, and actions like brushing a pony or feeding a rabbit can improve fine and gross motor skills. This can increase children's motivation to continue exercising muscles which might otherwise be neglected and provide a sense of achievement that might not be possible from completing other exercises.

Behaviour and Wellbeing

Perhaps more indirectly, introducing animals as a long-term classroom companion can have a calming effect, helping children regulate emotions and reduce stress.

Animals can increase overall motivation to attend and participate. Even reluctant learners may be tempted to participate more when an animal is involved, and we've talked already about the benefits of introducing an animal in reducing the pressure that a child might feel when communicating or interacting with a practitioner. Further to the direct impact of animals when they're introduced, the structured nature of activities with animals can help to develop routine, predictability and confidence, even when elements of the situation are, by nature, not always the same each time.

Example Use Cases for Cross-Curricular Integration

Mathematics

- Measuring and weighing food portions
- Calculating care costs
- Identifying patterns in animal features
- Time management for feeding and care schedules

Science

- Animal classification and characteristics
- Life cycles and development
- Habitat sludies
- Environmental adaptation

Language Arts

- Communication and vocabulary development
- Research and documentation skills
- Creative writing and storytelling
- Links with animal-themed art and literature

Physical Education

- Animal movement exploration
- Fine and gross motor skill development through animal care

- Active play and engagement
- Comparisons between animal and human anatomy

We'll explore these ideas in more depth as we build a case for animal-assisted education in this guide. We'll start with the 'big picture' and drill down, chapter by chapter, into the benefits, process, theory and practicalities of introducing animals into settings, scaffolded with case studies, practical examples and details of activities used in animal-assisted and traditional classroom settings to reap the benefits of animals in lessons.

As Helen Lewis and Russell Grigg (2020) highlight, animals 'can contribute towards learning in different subject areas and across the curriculum', underscoring just how versatile and far-reaching their impact can be, when the approach is right!

Animal-assisted education might seem unconventional, especially if you have concerns about space, and you might expect significant push-back when first introducing the idea of animals in the classroom.

This guide aims to provide comprehensive support to help you to build and contextualise your case for animals in your setting, starting with the basics as a sort of 'executive summary' for our proposal. (We'll cover what a successful executive study might need to include

Figure 1.10 Space concerns can limit possibilities, but Colin the African Land Snail doesn't take up much space at all

later, when we look at the 'business studies' bit of the guide, where we'll talk about how to build a business case.)

Next up, we'll look more closely at those psychological impacts and why it's so important to get the introduction of animals right, in order to benefit from the psychological safety and sensory benefits of animal assistance, before we move on to considering the more practical elements of your project.

2

Animal Therapy in Action
The Psychological Power of Animals in Education Settings

> The emotional benefits of interacting with animals can be profound, particularly in educational settings where stress and anxiety can impede learning. This chapter explores the theory and explains how animals can decrease cortisol levels, increase oxytocin and foster an environment where students feel safe, cared for and able to learn.

In the first chapter, we talked a little bit about the psychological impacts that animals can have on children's ability to learn and develop new skills, but the psychological benefits of introducing animals to your setting can be far wider-reaching than that. Animals have an innate ability to connect with us on an emotional level, which anyone who's ever had a dog can see for themselves. Man's best friend didn't get his name through lack of emotional bonding!

Regulating Emotions Through Animal Interactions

How Animals Help Children Feel Safe, Seen and Ready to Learn

Digging further into ideas around the psychological benefits of animals at school, it's been shown that when students spend time with animals, be it through petting, feeding or just watching them, there's a noticeable drop in cortisol, the stress hormone, and a corresponding rise in oxytocin, known as the 'love hormone'. Research tells us that such interactions can alleviate depression, boost happiness and even help manage symptoms of attention deficit hyperactivity disorder (ADHD) in children and young people through increased co-regulation.

As Vanfleet and Faa-Thompson (2010) explain, 'neurobiology has shown that the production of oxytocin in humans is stimulated by interactions with animals, creating the potential for greater relaxation and increased empathy and engagement'. In fact, studies suggest that interacting with animals can significantly lower stress and anxiety for everyone involved, not only the learners.

16 Animal-Assisted Learning

Figure 2.1 Animals can form strong bonds with humans, just ask St Luke's school budgie!

Figure 2.2 Walter is a great example of why dogs are known as 'man's best friend'

Integrating animals into education has some obvious reasons for working. They can help to lighten the mood and give people something to focus on, for example. But spending time with animals also helps to build resilience. Caring for animals helps to teach responsibility, empathy and patience among other core skills. The same child who gives up easily when confronted with a dexterity exercise might spend time working to close a lock or restock fiddly food dishes, and feeding hungry but clumsy bottle lambs provides regular opportunities to practise patience and empathy.

Regulating Emotions Through Animal Interactions

Almost all of the skills we need to thrive can be developed with support from animals. Animals don't judge us in the same way that other humans might, and they respond to emotions in a way that can teach children and young people to identify and react positively and safely to different feelings in both themselves and others. This can be particularly beneficial for students in care or educational settings who might need a boost in social interaction, or who struggle with empathy or communication.

As Birkett (2023) notes, 'introducing animals into the life of a child with SEN… the actions of stroking… can calm an anxious child very quickly', showing how even simple interactions can have a powerful emotional impact. For children, especially those with special educational needs, animals can help to turn a school into a safe, comforting place. Animals being present can help to reduce sensory overload by giving students a focal point for calm, and when managing emotions is the focus, animals can provide a live lesson in self-regulation.

Calming a nervous animal can teach children techniques that they can use to soothe their own anxieties, and learning to co-regulate with animals is a brilliant way to build that same ability with other people.

This might be achieved by asking children to stop and observe the animals' behaviour, and try to assess what the animal might be feeling, or teaching children about how feelings can be 'caught' through the way that we give off our own signals, with animals reacting to playful behaviour or becoming calm when children are calm. One of the benefits of this sort of demonstration is that it gives us the opportunity to demonstrate breathwork techniques (even showing just how a big breath out can help relax us and the animals) and mindfulness options as a route to co-regulating with the animals. Being quiet can help nervous animals and children… and playful animals can help us to feel happy.

Therapeutic Application Focus

Animal-Assisted Therapy in Action

Jenny's work in special educational needs and disabilities (SEND) settings has shown how animals being introduced to classrooms can lead to significant changes. In her animal-focused teaching, learners who have been diagnosed as autistic and who find transitions challenging have adapted much more easily when animal care is part of their day. The

18 Animal-Assisted Learning

Figure 2.3 Small animals, like Serenity the Hamster, can help to instill a sense of calm

Figure 2.4 Co-regulation is supported by rats and other furry friends who need quiet and calm to feel safe

animals offer a steady, comforting presence that aids in smoother transitions, helping children to find a sense of safety and familiarity when everything else is changing.

Learners (and educators) of all ages can struggle with anxiety and depression. The world is changing quickly, and there's a 24-hour news cycle, myriad hormones in play, pressure-cooker environments and all of the other pressures that have always existed in the classroom. This uncertainty means that sometimes it can be difficult to find stability, even for grown-ups, and animals can serve as a bridge back to normalcy, offering a form of therapeutic interaction that traditional teaching might not reach, and which can be instrumental in helping learners to feel connected and calm again, ready to play and learn.

We say play *and* learn, but play is an essential part of learning. It's at the heart of childhood and, in the UK, it's deemed so important that a yearly event celebrates children's right to play. Celebrated annually on the first Wednesday of August, National Playday is coordinated by a number of play-focused organisations and positions play as a fundamental right for children because of its importance in children's lives and development.

That's because play is not just an activity; it's a fundamental process through which children engage with the world, develop social skills and make sense of their environment. It's self-motivating, enjoyable and a means rather than an end. With play, the journey is as

Figure 2.5 Goats love to be friendly and enjoy playing with humans

Figure 2.6 Pigs are very intelligent and can be surprisingly playful

important as the destination, and people (and animals) of all ages engage in play to be creative, solve problems and learn new things.

When animals are part of this play, they can help to amplify its educational and psychological benefits, just through being there, and this can embody many of the key characteristics of play:

- **Active engagement:** Running with a dog or mimicking animal movements allows children to incorporate physical activity into their play without it feeling like a chore, stimulating both body and mind, and supporting active living and the enjoyment of stimulating screen-free time.
- **Meaningful interaction:** Children having the opportunity to learn and understand care for other beings helps to foster empathy and responsibility, and helps children to develop their emotional intelligence.
- **Symbolic play:** Animals can be central characters in imaginative scenarios, from being a vet to a farmer – children get to experiment in a number of animal-focused roles, try new personas and explore the skills and traits of different careers.
- **Voluntary and self-directed:** Once animals are embedded into a setting, children may be able to choose more freely how they engage with animals, and learn to express their discomfort or concerns, promoting autonomy and self-regulation.

- **Pleasure and intrinsic motivation:** The joy of interacting with animals can help to encourage children to repeat these experiences, deepening learning all around and helping to embed the animals into future learning, increasing their opportunities to make an impact.
- **Process-oriented:** When working with animals, the focus is often on the interaction itself, not on achieving specific outcomes. This nurtures children's creativity and exploration skills through removing the feeling of being tested or needing to 'measure up'. Even when assessment is the aim, the focus on an animal or process can remove pressure and allow children to thrive in their completion of tasks and explorations.
- **Adventurous and risk-taking:** Learning to interact with different animals teaches children to assess and manage risk, which is a vital life skill. Continual assessment is vital when working with animals, and teaching children to be aware of their surroundings, to stay present in the moment and to perceive hazards and risks can help to embed safety and teach independence.

Animals in Emotional and Physical Therapy

From a psychological perspective, animals can help as part of the provision of safe and non-judgemental spaces for children to experiment with identity, emotions and social roles.

Animal-assisted settings are arenas where children can practise resilience, learn to cope with setbacks (e.g. an animal not responding as expected) and grow in confidence and self-esteem alongside their animal friends. This form of play is not just for children... Adults, too, can benefit from the stress-reducing (and joy-enhancing!) qualities of animal-assisted play, as seen in the growing number of goat yoga classes, cow-cuddling experiences and alpaca-walking opportunities being advertised across the country.

Animals don't judge, remember?

Guy Claxton developed the concept of learning blocks, which are a set of psychological skills that enable a learner to engage effectively with a multitude of learning challenges, and which help to explain some of what we mean when we talk about how animals can scaffold play and learning. Claxton expressed that these blocks help children to develop a form of intelligence so that they are then able to, as Jean Piaget said, 'know what to do when they don't know what to do' (Costa and Kallick, 2000).

While the psychological benefits of engagement with friendly animals has been recognised and understood, animal-assisted therapy has also been shown to improve participants' social, emotional and cognitive functioning. And due to the successes demonstrated by existing animal-assisted experience providers, animal-assisted therapy is becoming more popular and increasingly utilised by occupational therapists, physiotherapists and speech and language therapists, with specific, focused therapeutic aims and objectives in mind.

Physiotherapy, for example, is a form of therapy which relies on patient motivation and is most successful when patients complete their full course of therapy. By incorporating animals into therapy sessions, children – and people in general – are often more willing to participate as they find the process fun and see the purpose and immediate payoff of their increased effort. Incorporating animals into the delivery of physiotherapy or exercise can be helpful in many different ways; generally, animal-assisted therapy creates a willingness and increased motivation to achieve identified therapy goals and targets.

For patients with neurological complications, there can be multiple benefits of engaging with animals through grooming, walking/exercise and care routines such as feeding, watering and cleaning. These can include helping with posture control, sitting and standing, encouraging focus and attention to stimulate awareness of the affected (weaker) side, and promoting speech and language development in a non-judgemental environment. These activities can also develop a patient's sequencing and memory skills.

Psychologically, there are multiple things at play here. Aside from providing motivation, repetitive, goal-oriented movements such as brushing an animal or walking a dog encourage neuroplasticity, which is the brain's ability to rewire itself by forming new neural connections. Animals, especially moving ones, naturally draw attention, so when a dog walks or turns to the patient's affected side, the patient is encouraged to orient toward that side, encouraging natural boundary stretching and physical recovery.

Because of this, those patients with walking and mobility difficulties might be more willing to engage in exercises and walking practice when given the task of walking an animal to ensure the animal gets the exercise it needs. Motivation to complete exercise for its own sake, even when the benefits are obvious, can be difficult to find, and results might seem far away and intangible. In contrast, the happiness, gratitude and love a canine companion might provide as reward for walking is immediate and fulfilling.

Dogs have even been trained to function as mobility stability aids by walking closely at a person's side (generally the side that is weaker) to provide support to them. To achieve this, the dog's height and weight need to be considered together with the patient's height and weight, and this sort of pairing should always be guided by a trained professional, but the impact can be incredible. Even when not offering physical support, the presence of the dog can give people more confidence, more determination and more motivation to walk further or more regularly.

The Therapeutic Impact of Fur, Scales and Feathers

We've already talked about how children who need support to develop their fine and gross motor skills and/or muscle control in their arms and or legs can be stimulated to participate by offering them the opportunity to groom an animal. As they work and play, the manipulation of grooming equipment will develop their motor skills, and the brushing movement and motions will develop their muscle control in their arms and hands, while also helping

Figure 2.7 Stoking and grooming animals, such as rabbits, can help children to develop fine and gross motor skills

to develop their coordination and pressure manipulation skills. Walking these animals to a grooming space from their personal area will also support the development of these skills.

Fine notes that 'tactile contact with animals like rabbits and llamas has been linked with reductions in cortisol levels and improved mood in therapeutic settings' (2010, p. 134), showing that the sensory and emotional impact of such interactions can be as powerful as the physical.

Through this interaction, these patients experience an enhancement in their communication ability, play and social skills, and can also be found to develop their own self-care skills after having cared for another living being.

Lessons from Dementia Care Practice

While this guide is primarily designed to support educators working with children, one of the ways that the benefits of animal-assisted education have been evidenced is through its deployment in the dementia care arena. Cats and dogs are the most popular choice in these projects, and a German study running for six months found that animal interaction improved social behaviours, improved verbal communication functions and supported greater attentiveness in the cohort that was followed (Wesenburg et al., 2019). In addition to this research, a study at the University of Nebraska's College of Nursing found patients exhibited fewer symptoms of sundown syndrome, which can be a particularly distressing condition associated with dementia that occurs in the early evening and involves behaviours such as restlessness, confusion, wandering, hitting and kicking. Therapy dogs attending care homes in the early evening tended to distract the patients and appeared to relax

Figure 2.8 Chinchillas can be a popular nostalgic pet amongst older learners

them when they might usually experience these symptoms, reducing the impact of sundown syndrome and providing relief when it might be needed most (University of Nebraska Medical Center, 2022).

Perhaps because these patients are older, it has been found that ferrets and tortoises are also popular, as they were common pets in the 1950s and 1960s. It's possible that bringing back memories of childhood is a factor in their popularity, and possibly in their ability to create a positive impact. Chinchillas have also been found to elicit good responses, as some of the patients remember them and may recall memories of chinchilla fur coats and other social changes that have the potential to spark conversation and nostalgia.

Animals, regardless of the species classification, seem to have a positive effect on the experiences of dementia patients in a variety of ways. As Birkett (2023) notes, 'therapy animals… can include hens, fish, reptiles and insects too', reminding us that therapeutic benefit isn't limited to the traditional cats and dogs.

At the very least, animals lift people's spirits, allow them to experience anticipation of their arrival, bring a smile and produce a laugh, all of which is good medicine for the body, mind and soul.

Substance Dependence Syndrome Treatment

Imagine a world where patients in rehab can walk up to a community animal and pet it to calm their anxieties or beat their relapse cravings, or where parents and children who have experienced substance abuse and its impacts on relationships and social norms can bond and learn together with the help of an animal to focus on.

Substance-dependent patients might focus exclusively on themselves as part of their dependency or their recovery, and engagement with animals can encourage them to more easily think of others and their needs. Therapy delivered within a group can allow people to interact socially with others and, as in other use cases we've already discussed, it's likely that people might be more likely to interact or join in with group sessions if animals are involved.

Alongside this benefit, animal interactions can provide additional opportunities for clinical observation and interaction. Doctors who have observed dependent patients interacting with animals have a greater opportunity to gain insight into the patient's self-esteem and might be able to identify specific coping mechanisms and healthier emerging behaviours through observing people when they're less guarded and interacting with the animal instead of the therapist directly.

This research and insight relates directly to our work in the classroom., showing how animals can introduce fun to therapy and classroom settings as well as providing and facilitating lessons in team work, communication, trust and self-expression.

Skunks and Schizophrenia

When considering which animals have been shown to support people in different situations, the most impactful animals can be surprising. For example, it's been found that patients with paranoid schizophrenia might benefit from spending time interacting with skunks. Skunks are the same shape and size as a cat, but are more likely to want to cuddle than cats and are much less choosy about their companions, allowing those who might have experienced rejection or rejection sensitivity to avoid further damage to their self-esteem and start to build relationships, which will allow them to build resilience to try other interactions that may include the risk of rejection.

Because skunks are quite social, patients are able to stroke skunks more freely than they might be able to with a cat, releasing endorphins while also having a calming effect on them. Although you may be concerned about the stink that a skunk might bring, practitioners and caretakers need not worry about their famously unpleasant smell. Skunks only release this when they fear they are about to die, and we'd certainly hope that this is never a possibility when they're safe, loved and cared for. Skunks are actually a very clean animal, and if they're not feeling a huge threat, they smell just like cats! Skunks will also provide all the other physiological, emotional and cognitive benefits that other animal interactions might provide. Who would have thought it?

This not only shows the impact that might be made through the introduction of unlikely animals, but also demonstrates how important it is to spend time properly considering which animals might be right for your setting, the children who attend it and, perhaps most importantly, for the animals themselves.

Animal Support in Narrative Therapy

Connections and companionships can be formed with the most unlikely of animals, and, if appropriate, this additional lens might support other lessons and subject planning, opening the door for educators to explore themes like stereotyping, prejudice, etiquette and social norms. As John Winslade and Gerald Monk so clearly put it, 'The problem is the problem. The person is not the problem' (1999, p. 2). Helping us to understand this, animals can support us to depersonalise problems and work them through less confrontationally.

Animal-assisted metaphor and storytelling is growing in popularity. Animal stories, pictures and metaphors are utilised as symbols to reflect a person's experiences to support them in gaining insight and growth through separating the person from a problem and allowing them to externalise their problems instead of internalising them. Stories can function as a distraction and help to get around a person's resistance and defences by depersonalising the telling of the story. The person is able to more easily relate to the image, story or metaphor while feeling less threatened because it is not being expressed or presented as a personal issue but instead framed as something that's happening to someone else, someone who might even be fictional.

Figure 2.9 Animals, like Tyson the rabbit, can help people with storytelling

This opens up lots of opportunities to introduce animals into settings incrementally. Whether you're concerned about providing space for animals and your ability to care for the animals in your setting long term, or you're looking for the best ways to assess the way that the children in your setting might react to animals when they're face to face for the first time, working with stories and pictures can be a great way to introduce animals as a focus and to begin to build children's understanding of emotional intelligence, self-regulation and risk assessment.

Successful outcomes in animal-assisted narrative therapy are based on the principle that while the images shown briefly shift the focus onto the animal, the person generally tends to process the animal's experience or story through their person perspective, which is based and formed around their own life experiences.

The process allows a person to imagine what the animal is experiencing and facilitates the person to tap more deeply into their suppressed and, in some cases, even repressed feelings and experiences. Animal-assisted narrative diverts a person's guarded self-awareness and facilitates access where it is normally limited through the use of more directive inquiry and might allow exploration of deeper themes like bullying, isolation and belonging.

As a bonus, it can be facilitated in a number of different ways, both directly with live animals and through pictures, videos and other remote animal interactions.

Narrative therapy is:

- **Respectful** and places importance on respecting everyone's dignity. It views each person as an individual who can't be deficient, defective or not 'enough' in any way.
- **Non-blaming**, where people are not blamed for the problems they are experiencing and they are also encouraged not to blame others.

A Bridge to Connection

Narrative therapy separates problems from people and sees the person as a functional, whole person who engages in thought and/or behaviour patterns that they would like to change.

Children's problems can sometimes be compounded by the inability of the adults in their lives to understand and respond effectively to the children's feelings and their attempts at communicating these feelings to them. The resulting 'communication gap' might then be further widened as a result of the adult's insistence that children use those expressions used commonly by adults themselves or when adults are unable to find the subtext in children's expression.

Play is a very natural form of communication and one that children use instinctually to express themselves, where adults might often utilise verbalisation as their preferred method.

Since their language development is slower than their cognitive development, children might express their awareness of what is taking place within their world through their play. Play therapy can utilise animals as being part of the children's world and their play, and form part of the child's recognised and respected language.

Emotionally significant experiences can then be expressed more comfortably and safely within and through the symbolic representation that animals (or animal images and animal-shaped toys) can provide. Once this is established, children might then transfer the expression of anxieties, fears, guilt and fantasies on to and through objects and animals instead of people. Throughout the process, children can often feel safer and more secure in their own feelings and reactions, as their play enables them to separate themselves from any traumatic experiences and events that might otherwise inform their interactions. This can mean that children can be prevented from feeling the overwhelm that they might otherwise experience from expressing their memories or emotions, as the act takes place within the realm of fantasy.

By reproducing and acting out frightening or traumatic experiences and even possibly changing and reversing outcomes through play, children might be able to move towards an inner resolution that enables them to cope better with their problems or adjust to them.

There are different approaches towards play therapy, some being more non-directive and person centred, while others are more directive. Play therapy and animals have a natural connection, and among the normal play therapy toys available in a setting, there should be a selection of toys with animal themes, such as puppets, masks and figures, as well as a range of appropriate items for the animal to be engaged with in therapeutic interventions, such as grooming brushes, blankets and toys. Animals offer what's often described as a 'social lubricant effect', helping those who find it difficult to trust or connect with others to engage more freely and comfortably.

As Ford Sori and Ciastko Hughes (2014) reflect, 'there's something that happens when the animal is there, perhaps it creates an additional sense of safety, perhaps less focus on the child, less self-consciousness… That forms a bridge to improved human connections.' This captures the essence of animal-assisted play therapy, which is firmly grounded in attachment theory and uses the animal's presence to gently encourage the building of trust, safety and relational engagement.

3

Introducing Children to Animals and Farm Therapy (A Process)

> Introducing animals into educational environments requires a thoughtful process. From selecting the right animals to match educational goals to preparing students for interaction, this chapter outlines step-by-step strategies. It includes how to manage first encounters, build trust and ensure both student and animal welfare are maintained throughout the educational journey.

Now that we have a grounding in the theory and an understanding of how animals can provide benefits within educational settings and practices, you might be thinking, 'Well, that's all very well and good, but none of this helps me to make it happen' – and you'd be right! It's important to examine some of the theory behind *why* animal therapy in education might be beneficial for children and grown-ups, but this book isn't a theoretical exercise. We promised that we'd contextualise and make tangible animal-assisted education, and that starts in this chapter.

From here, we'll explore how you can introduce animals in your setting, from selecting the right animals to getting a budget and the permissions to get started, as well as the support to keep going.

If you haven't got one already, now might be a good time to grab a notebook and your favourite pen (or to open your computer). We're going to start building our own plans and developing our ideas in our own context.

Laying the Groundwork

Understanding Your Goals

When starting out, it's important to first ask yourself what outcomes you are hoping for. Are you looking for support from animals with improved emotional regulation, the development of empathy and increased educational engagement, or for opportunities to develop children's sense of responsibility or their communication through the introduction of this tangible learning?

DOI: 10.4324/9781003649304-3

Which children will benefit most from the changes, and why?

Is it that children with anxiety, those who are diagnosed as autistic or those with low confidence, a trauma history or cognitive disabilities might benefit from the interactions we've talked about in the first two chapters? What changes would you like to see in the way they're able to interact? Are there more specific educational outcomes you're looking for? Is mathematics a key area you're looking to scaffold and contextualise, for example, or are soft skills more important?

Knowing what you'd like to achieve for the children in your care is the most important aspect of planning your animal interactions and deciding how best to introduce animals to your setting.

 Spend some time reflecting on your current class and their needs. We're going to define some objectives for our animal project and some key results, which will tell us how we're doing against those goals. Setting Objectives and Key Results helps us to define what the project might need to look like in order to meet these objectives and helps us to communicate our project aims to others, including demonstrating transparency and the alignment of our project with any organisational or regional goals for children's wellbeing, education and development.

Ask yourself what values you want this programme to reflect. Is kindness to animals high up on your list? The development of patience? An introduction to sensory regulation for children? Curiosity? Or shared responsibility?

If you were inspired, or even overwhelmed, by the number of ways that animals might be able to make a difference in your setting, you might find that you have a lot of ideas about what you'd like to achieve, but it's important not to choose too many objectives. Yes, animals can have a far-reaching impact, but choosing too many objectives is almost guaranteed to reduce your focus and dilute the impact of your provision.

Try to choose the three objectives that are most important to you and the children you support. Ask yourself: 'Am I looking for therapeutic intervention or a broader educational enhancement?' and set up your objectives as smart goals, such as: 'By the end of term, participating students will demonstrate improved peer cooperation skills during animal care routines.'

Decide how you'll measure your progress against your goals.

Taking our example from above, if we are to see students demonstrate improved peer cooperation, we'll need to measure where they are now and set out what might be considered an improvement. How will you measure this improvement? How many learners would need to demonstrate this improvement for you to consider this a success?

As an example, when written out as an Objective and Key Results (OKRs), this goal might change to look like this.

Objective: Foster stronger peer cooperation skills among students during animal care routines.
Key result 1: 80 per cent of participating students demonstrate improved cooperation skills as observed during animal care activities by the end of term.
Key result 2: At least three peer-led animal care tasks are successfully completed each week without adult intervention.
Key result 3: 90 per cent of students receive positive peer feedback on cooperation at least once during the term.
Key result 4: Incidents of peer conflict during animal care routines are reduced by 50 per cent compared to the start of term.

Repeat this exercise for your three chosen goals and don't be scared to change your mind as you explore and reflect. One of the benefits of planning in this way is that we can properly spend time iterating and developing our ideas until they're ambitious and achievable, with measurements of success built in. We'd do the process a disservice if we decided to storm ahead with the first three things that popped into our head.

You now have three objectives that can be attained through the introduction of animals and a way to measure them, and these will form the foundation of every other decision we make as our planning, and then our project, progresses.

Bringing the Vision to Life

Choosing the Right Animals

You might, by this stage of reading, be keen to get to the animal planning.

It would be unusual to get this far without having developed some sort of picture of the sort of setting we might like to achieve. Whether you're thinking about introducing a class dog, a couple of horses or a guinea-pig enclosure, try to take a step back and stay open-minded. We're going to be led by the OKRs we've set and look at which animals might best support these aims and, on the other hand, how these aims might conflict with the needs of any animal that we might consider. And, as part of this, we still need to give serious consideration to the question of whether a permanent animal programme is right for your objectives, or whether other provision or projects wouldn't be better suited to what you'd like to achieve.

For example, guinea pigs are often suggested for younger children or residential settings. As Fine points out, 'guinea pigs' calm and predictable nature make them ideal for therapy with young children and elderly populations, helping reduce stress and promote relaxation' (2010, p. 147). Patty Born Selly adds that 'their small size and ease of care facilitate their use in educational and therapeutic settings, encouraging nurturing behaviours' (2014, pp. 55-65). They're low maintenance in comparison to larger animals, but still offer consistent opportunities for interaction, empathy and routine.

Dogs are often a popular choice. Their sensitivity to human emotion and their capacity for companionship can make them powerful partners for supporting emotional regulation, building communication skills and helping children feel safe and valued. As McCune et al. note, 'dogs' unique ability to read human social cues supports their use in a wide range of psychological therapies, including for PTSD [post-traumatic stress disorder], anxiety, and depression' (2014, p. 34). But dogs are also complex animals with high social and physical needs. Dogs require structured downtime, careful supervision, and someone present who can reliably advocate for their welfare throughout the school day. Without the right planning and capacity, even a friendly classroom dog can become overwhelmed – and overwhelming.

Horses and ponies can offer rich, relationship-based learning, especially for children working on emotional regulation or recovering from trauma. Equines mirror human emotion and provide strong metaphorical teaching moments, which can offer learners the chance to build confidence, learn boundaries and develop trust.

As Chandler explains, 'equine-assisted therapy promotes emotional regulation, social skills, and physical coordination by engaging individuals in riding, grooming, and ground activities with horses' (2012, p. 57). Tedeschi and Jenkins add that 'therapeutic riding has shown to decrease anxiety, improve self-esteem, and support trauma recovery across ages' (2019, p. 102). Providing a project which includes horses isn't an entry-level option and might not be suitable for most schools or settings but, in the right environment and with the right support, equine partnerships can be deeply rewarding.

Small mammals such as rabbits or guinea pigs can be a gentler starting point. They're well suited for one-to-one interaction, especially for younger children or those with sensory processing needs, and their size and temperament make them ideal for lap-based or quiet handling activities. That said, these animals still require more care than many people assume. Rabbits, for example, need social contact, space to roam and enrichment to avoid stress. Many hutches advertised to buy online are much too small for the average rabbit, and they can easily become frightened if handled too frequently or without due care.

It's also worth remembering that a wide variety of small mammals, not just the familiar ones, can have therapeutic value. As Vanfleet and Faa-Thompson note, 'in small animal-assisted therapy programs, ferrets can enhance motivation and reduce feelings of isolation' (2018, p. 94), showing how even less conventional choices can bring meaningful connection and emotional support when thoughtfully integrated into a setting.

Introducing Children to Animals and Farm Therapy (A Process) 33

Figure 3.1 Chickens can be an excellent choice for companionship and observation

Figure 3.2 When handled as chicks, you can build trust and affection with chickens

Chickens can provide opportunities for routine-based learning and support work around responsibility, empathy and observation. They're excellent for group activities such as feeding and collecting eggs, and they can become part of wider curriculum learning in subjects such as science and food education. Did you know that chickens are descendants of the T-Rex? They are better suited to settings with outdoor space, as chickens are much happier when they can roam outdoors, and they're generally more comfortable being observed than handled, so activities need to be carefully structured around that. If you raise chickens from eggs, you'll find that handling them early helps to build their trust when being picked up. While this might increase their tolerance for pets and cuddles, it's also a great way to make health checks and hygiene interventions much less stressful for the chickens and for you. Selby and Wright highlight that 'handling chickens provides multi-sensory stimulation and encourages responsibility, which can reduce agitation in older adults and enhance concentration in children with special needs' (2014, p. 48), pointing to their value across a broad age and ability range. Likewise, McGee et al. found that 'the responsibility of caring for birds fosters routine and engagement in children and adults with mental health challenges' (2018, p. 102), further reinforcing their potential as both educational companions and emotional anchors.

Speaking of dinosaur descendants, reptiles may not be the first animals that come to mind, but they offer a valuable point of difference, particularly for learners who are drawn to the unusual or who experience sensory challenges. Many reptiles are slow-moving and enjoy warm handling environments, which can have a calming effect on children. They also present fewer allergen concerns than furry or feathered animals, and offer visual interest without the noise levels associated with mammals or birds.

As Fine notes, 'reptiles, such as turtles and lizards, offer unique sensory experiences and can help reduce fear responses in phobic individuals' (2010, p. 162), making them a potential asset in specialised therapeutic contexts. And while they might show less outward emotional expression, their calm presence and relatively low maintenance needs make them suitable in the right circumstances. However, they do have very specific care requirements, especially in terms of heating, diet and hygiene, so doing your research is important!

We've talked a little bit about farm therapy, and it's true that farm animals such as goats, sheep and cows can provide multi-sensory, inclusive learning experiences. They are particularly well suited to outdoor settings and can support curriculum areas from science to food technology, as well as broader personal development. As Morris and Lewis observe, 'gentle interaction with sheep through grooming and herding activities contributes to stress reduction and develops motor skills and empathy' (2017, p. 23), underlining their value for both emotional and physical learning.

But there's also a lot more decision making to do here. Different breeds offer different possibilities – there's not just 'a sheep' or 'a goat' – and just like different breeds of dogs, each will have its own benefits and drawbacks in any given scenario. As a rule, smaller animals

Introducing Children to Animals and Farm Therapy (A Process) 35

Figure 3.3 Snakes can be a good option for a classroom pet when allergies are a concern

like pygmy goats are easier to manage physically, while larger animals like cows or ponies offer opportunities for more embodied or physical learning. Their care, however, is continuous and demanding, requiring access to land, shelter and veterinary support. You'll also need to look into the additional requirements that you might face if you choose to keep livestock. You may find that you need special licences, or need to take additional steps to register your animals, such as through any mandatory leg-ringing, tagging or tattooing schemes.

Insects and other small creatures can be a wonderful place to start, especially for settings with limited space or those just beginning their animal-assisted journey. Stick insects, snails and beetles are low maintenance and can be observed closely, supporting science learning and curiosity without the complexity of the care associated with mammals. They also offer gentle exposure for children who are anxious around animals and might help you to 'start small' and show the benefits and potential of animal-assisted learning before making the case for more animals, space or time.

Figure 3.4 Some animals might require additional registration or training. Doing your research is important

Step by Step

Designing Ethical, Effective Animal-Assisted Provision

Go back to your goals and consider what kind of animal provision might be best to meet these needs. Remember, starting with a time-bound project or choosing to work with an outside agency to provide animal interactions now doesn't mean you can't build from here and complete other, longer or more permanent or complex projects in the future.

Options for different types of provision might be wider-ranging than you first think. It's definitely not 'all or nothing' when it comes to implementing projects which involve animals, and you might wish to combine approaches, such as working with a local rare-breed chicken breeder to run a hatching project at school and a visit to the farm to meet the chickens when they're older, or regular updates from 'your' chicks once they're back at home.

Figure 3.5 Raising chicks can be a great learning experience, but what happens when they're fully grown?

Matching Provision to Children's Needs

There are so many ways to bring animals into your education setting, and they all have their own benefits, limitations and considerations. What's important is that your provision fits the goals you've already set, the needs of your children and the realities of your setting's capacity.

One of the most accessible starting points is working with a visiting provider. These are organisations or individuals who bring animals into school settings for short sessions, often focused on wellbeing, curriculum learning or a themed event. This could be a mobile farm, a reptile experience or a visit from a therapy dog and their handler. These visits can bring joy, excitement and learning, particularly for children who may not otherwise have access to animal experiences at home, and you'll benefit from an expert animal facilitator to learn from and observe. For those reasons, this option can be a gentle way in, minimising the burden of care or planning, while still observing how children respond. However, the impact of these sessions often depends on how well they are embedded into wider learning, and how thoughtfully they're framed. Without preparation and follow-up, visits can feel like a novelty, rather than part of an integrated learning journey. It's also vital that the providers you work with uphold the same standards of ethics, safeguarding and welfare as your setting would expect from itself.

You might also consider taking children out of school to visit animals in their own environments. Trips to farms, animal sanctuaries or nature-based education centres offer a different kind of opportunity to immerse ourselves in the animals' space and context with real curiosity. In these settings, animals are typically kept in well-adapted environments, giving children the opportunity to observe natural behaviours and learn about how animals are cared for day-to-day. This kind of provision can be particularly powerful when linked to curriculum areas like science, food education or geography, or used to support emotional and social development through calm, sensory-rich experiences. Practical challenges such as transport, cost and accessibility can pose barriers, so it's worth thinking about whether repeat visits are possible, or if you can build relationships with local providers who might welcome regular contact as you consider your own provision.

If you're ready for something a little more hands-on, time-bound projects can offer a wonderful bridge between visiting provision and a permanent responsibility. Projects like chick hatching, caterpillar-to-butterfly cycles or even looking after stick insects allow learners to experience the rhythm of animal life in a safe and structured way. These types of projects are ideal for introducing responsibility and routine, and they offer rich learning opportunities around life cycles, observation and emotional regulation. Because they're temporary, they can also serve as a manageable first step into animal provision. Although simpler to

Figure 3.6 External visits can provide opportunities to see animals in their natural environment

Introducing Children to Animals and Farm Therapy (A Process) 39

Figure 3.7 City farms can be a great place to meet animals that you might not usually see up close

initiate than forever provision, shorter-term projects still require careful planning. Animals need daily care, even over weekends and holidays, and endings need to be managed with care, especially if children form emotional bonds with the animals involved. Done well, these time-limited interactions can provide a springboard into deeper work and might lead to permanent provision or culminate in a trip out to see the animals in their forever home.

We've already covered how permanent provision can support everything from daily routines to curriculum learning and therapeutic intervention. Children benefit from the consistency, and over time, they develop meaningful relationships with the animals, learning how to interpret behaviour, manage emotions and take ownership for care tasks. But this kind of provision also demands significant ongoing commitment. You'll need to plan for care outside of school hours, respond to veterinary needs and ensure that all staff understand their roles in keeping animals safe and comfortable. It's a big investment, but one that can offer profound rewards when rooted in ethics and shared responsibility.

Some schools choose to collaborate with external partners on a more regular basis, creating hybrid models of provision. This might mean working with a local animal-assisted practitioner who visits weekly, developing a partnership with a care farm for sustained pupil placements, or linking up with a rare-breed breeder to follow the journey of a particular animal. These ongoing partnerships can offer a lovely balance of consistency and professional expertise, allowing your learners to form relationships with animals and practitioners, without needing to house or care for animals full-time yourselves. As with all collaborative work, clear communication, shared values, and well-documented safeguarding and welfare expectations are essential.

No matter which path you choose, the key is to contextualise the decision within your own setting's needs and strengths. There's no requirement to leap straight into permanent provision or to commit to something that feels overwhelming. Start by asking what your learners need most right now, and what your team can sustainably support. Would a simple egg-hatching project help to build interest? Could a visit from a therapy dog pave the way for something more regular? Are there local providers or farm settings who would be willing to partner with you?

Start with Why

You Don't Have to Do It All at Once

Whether now is the right time for a permanent introduction or not, the first way that we'll introduce animals to our learners is the same. We want learners to be prepared to meet their new companions and to know what to expect. It's helpful for learners to have at least a basic understanding of health and safety around the animals, and it can be beneficial to warm up children emotionally too. New experiences can be overwhelming, and we don't always know when children might feel taken aback by changes or what their previous experiences with animals might look like.

This process can be a little frustrating, as it might introduce new hurdles to your eventual introduction. Finding out that children are allergic to your planned animal choice, encountering parental objections and understanding how animals will need to be housed and cared for might necessitate us revisiting our choice of animals or having another go at shaping our objectives. Try not to get too caught up in the plan until it's needed. Like the ongoing work that you're hoping to do with the animals, staying open to change and developing our own curiosity is important when developing the case for a successful project.

Prep and Parents

Before introducing animals to the classroom, it's important to properly understand the needs of the children in your class and, as part of this, to consider the things that only their parents might know. Children might not declare an allergy to horses, for example, when coming to school, but will need teachers to be aware if equine interactions are being considered. Usually, the only way to gather this information is to involve parents in your planning and research.

With your chosen animals and types of interaction in mind, consider what you might need to know about children to make it a success. There are lots of ways to involve parents at the beginning of your planning, such as sending home a survey or questionnaire, or holding a small parent event to workshop your ideas.

Some things you might want to consider alongside parents and guardians are whether the children in your care have any allergies or medical conditions that might be exacerbated by animals during visits or lessons where animals are present, if children have any fears or phobias, and if there are any immune conditions or sensitivities (distinct from allergies) that you might need to navigate.

It's important to bear in mind that people might not always know about allergies or sensitivities. If children haven't been in contact with animals, parents might not have any way to know how they might react. Asking about previous animal interactions might help you to plan or to anticipate where safety might be most assured. If children have other allergies, for example, keeping an epi-pen close by when they first meet animals can help to lessen the risk.

As part of your collaboration with parents, you might wish to take the opportunity to ask about any sensory issues or difficulties that you might need to be aware of. Some animals come complete with strong smells and others might be noisy.

Depending on your existing relationships with parents, this might also be a good opportunity to ask about cultural beliefs and considerations, and any support that parents might need to be able to provide suitable clothing for interactions with animals.

You might even wish to combine this activity with permission gathering. It's always a good idea to have parental permission when making big changes, and maybe even to recruit some parental volunteers!

Inviting parents as volunteers, whether in the classroom or during the holidays, does introduce some additional considerations. Some animals can cause issues for anyone who might be pregnant (such as sheep and goats), and adults might have their own allergies or sensitivities.

It's also important not to make promises to parents at this stage, and to be clear that you are exploring the idea of introducing animals, rather than raising their expectations before you get sign-off on your project, but having parents on board can only add weight to your business case and might help to lighten the load (or help to inform your decision on which approach to take).

Similarly, input from colleagues might help to shape your project, alleviate concerns about holiday cover and raise issues that you'll need to take into account in your planning.

So... you've got a list of suitable animals and some solid objectives, and your parents and colleagues are now involved in your planning. We're going to skip ahead a little now, but don't worry, we're just taking a break from the 'boring bits' and the admin while we consider how the transition from no animals to animals will work.

If you're enjoying your planning and project scoping, you can skip ahead again here and continue to plan with the support of Chapters 5 and 6, where we'll complete risk assessments and develop our project plan and business case.

Preparing Children for Animal Companions

Here, we'll continue with setting the scene for the children. Introducing animals doesn't start with the first interaction, but a long time before that, and building this into our planning will help us to create the impact that we're seeking much more effectively.

Before introducing animals into your setting, or even confirming that you're planning towards this, it's possible to use stories, photos, puppets and videos to create visual and emotional familiarity and to help to bring children along on the journey with you.

Think again about your objectives and key results. How will you choose content and activities that model the interactions you'd like to see? How might you be able to generate initial conversation about respect, personal space, self-regulation and diversity? Is there a local organisation or farm-park that could help you to introduce these ideas before you embark on your project? Now might be a good time to consider a visiting animal or trip out, or you might wish to start small. Many zoos and nature reserves have webcams that are accessible to the public. Can you use a live feed to help to introduce these conversations through observation tasks or an art lesson?

Once you get children talking, you can use these conversations to co-create class charters and social stories which model asking permission before touching, reading animal body language to understand how they're feeling, and being still and calm near animals to encourage co-regulation.

Keeping this preparation consistent and regular will help to build children's understanding and expectations of what to expect during animal encounters and can also be used to teach important concepts, develop soft skills and directly teach about animals and the natural world.

If you're looking for ideas for lessons that involve animals without them being present, head to Chapter 7, where we share activities, lesson ideas and case studies which might help you to introduce animal interactions, or even to provide positive animal experiences without live animals being part of your final plan.

Creating Safe Spaces for Learning with Animals

If and when it is time for first encounters, there are lots of ways to make the experience less overwhelming for both children and animals.

You might want to use gentle lighting, calm music and small group settings to establish sensory and emotional safety. Animals can be unpredictable and exciting, and we want to avoid overstimulation. We want to avoid unexpected noises or unannounced visits where possible, and to make sure that our animals and children feel safe and cared for in this new environment. Now is a crucial time, and it's important that we provide positive interactions to build on and to reduce the risk of children or animals developing fear about their engagement. When prepping our class for first contact, we can draw parallels with human feelings and animal behaviour through observation – 'Just like we need space when we're feeling overwhelmed, that's how a rabbit might be feeling when it hops away.'

An initial session where observation is the only objective can be a nice way to make first contact. Plan a session where children are tasked with counting how many times an animal does different actions (eating, jumping or making noises are good examples) and for them to make notes about the animal's temperament, likes and dislikes.

While this is an engaging and interactive plan for a session, it also allows time for your learners to adjust to the presence of the animals and for you to help to embed techniques for children to be able to assess animals temperaments and needs.

Starting with a small group structure (or, if it's right for your class, one-to-one sessions), we can start to spend time with the animals. Spending time in small groups can help lower the sensory load, give children space to feel their own feelings and allow adults to be aware of children's excitement or fear. Great ways to spend early sessions are still observation based. After your initial session, you could ask children to observe the animal's movements, record their sounds, monitor their body language and be curious. What questions do they have?

If you want to accelerate the acceptance of animals in your setting, incorporating animal themes into other lessons might also be helpful. Be creative. Food weights and measures can be introduced into maths sessions, creative writing and animal record-keeping can be incorporated into literacy, and your recorded animal noises might even help form the basis of a music workshop. Find existing songs that include animal references or help children to create their own, either through writing animal-based songs and poetry or using samples to create new tracks.

Whichever activities you plan into your first few weeks, spending time to help the children to understand co-regulation is important. By explaining that when they're calm, it helps the animals to be calm, children can make links between their behaviour and signalling and the things that they've observed in the animals, and can begin to anticipate how animals might react to various experiences and environments.

To support this, it can help to plan time to sit still together and model calm, slow breathing in the presence of your animal friends. Use a soft voice to narrate animal behaviour while the children breathe, and help the children to learn what animals might be thinking and feeling: 'She's sniffing because that's how she explores and learns.'

Validate children's emotions about learning and playing with animals: 'You're excited and so am I. Let's make sure we pay extra attention to how we're feeling and get calm so that we can show the guinea pig that she's safe with us.'

While this might seem slow and you might be keen to dive into using animals in every lesson, it's important to empower children with clear behavioural expectations, while maintaining the warm, supportive and curiosity-driven environment that you've been building. This can be difficult when working with animals and often requires empathy and an understanding of the situation, rather than clear control.

Developing children's awareness of risk, responsibility and the importance of empathetic encounters is key to making this work in practice.

Although each plan must differ in order to cater to the unique circumstances, needs and behaviours of your children and animals, there are some techniques we can apply to support children's ability to understand the boundaries of animal interaction and to set a good foundation for learning. Of course, there will always be some rules that can be very straightforward and clear cut – 'No spending time with the animals without an adult present' – but for many interactions, we'll need to swap our language and change 'you're not allowed to…' to 'our animal friends feel safe when…' to make sure that children understand why rules exist and to allow them to apply this learning to their own risk assessments and observations.

Reframing 'rules' in this way encourages empathy and helps children (and adults!) to connect to the reasons behind the rule, helping to establish why it's important and encourage the children to understand how one action can impact another. They're going to have to learn how to risk-assess situations alongside you, in order to feel comfortable predicting animal behaviour in the longer term. Asking children to consider their own bodily autonomy is another way to introduce or embed this, giving children the option to exercise their own personal boundaries during animal time: 'If you don't feel like being close today, that's OK. Watching quietly is part of being with the animals too.'

Building Routines

'Engaging in structured farm chores, such as feeding and cleaning, provides purposeful activity that supports recovery from addiction and mental health challenges by promoting routine and physical activity' (McGee, Townsend and Findling, 2018, p. 90).

Part of the magic of working with animals comes from the ability to build sustainable daily routines which support and encourage co-regulation, empathy and executive functioning. Starting the day, spending the time after lunch or ending the day with animal time can help

Introducing Children to Animals and Farm Therapy (A Process) 45

Figure 3.8 Learning to interpret animal behavior can help to keep learners safe, and support the development of emotional intelligence

build calm, predictable sessions for checking in with the animals, feeding, cleaning and spending quality time together. You've spent a lot of time thinking about how the children in your setting will respond to the animals, but being prepared for conflict between the children is also important. Think about how your children might need support to share roles, decide on turns and avoid tasks that are overwhelming. Depending on the needs of your class, you might use visual timetables or lanyards, and have fun names for roles like 'poop-scooper', 'observer' and 'comfort checker' which can be rotated periodically or chosen fresh every day. While it has to be OK for children to opt out of animal interaction to maintain a safe environment, there are lots of ways to encourage children to reflect on their interactions and feelings, and to empower children to try new things (or revisit things they've dismissed before). Try asking children to record animal observations or their feelings after an interaction. You can scaffold this with prompts like 'What did you notice today?' 'How do you think she felt when…' or 'What did you feel when you were with her?'

Maintaining the Environment

It might seem impossible, when you first introduce the animals, that it might become routine, but once it does, you can be sure that new challenges will arise. Once animals are settled, they will need enrichment activities to prevent them from becoming bored, in addition to their routine care. While we've already talked about keeping children's interest through routine and rotating jobs, animals will need toys, hiding spaces, foraging activities and other routine care, such as brushing or health checks, all dependent on the animal. You should have a good idea what sort of care and enrichment will support your animal from your initial research into the right animals for your setting and objectives. Revisiting these regularly can help you to spot signs of boredom or distress in your animal colleagues and allow you to make changes before problems arise.

Use these opportunities to teach children why these things matter. Why does a dog need to have its teeth brushed? Why might a chicken need a nail trim? What behaviours does this particular toy encourage for the pig? It might be possible to link this care to other parts of your curriculum.

Look back at your goals and try to find ways to meet your objectives using these regular touchpoints for animal care.

Making the Leap from Learning to Doing

To help keep your momentum, and to make your invisible learning visible across your school, you might want to employ some whole-school strategies and proudly show your class's emotional development alongside their academic progress.

Figure 3.9 When might a chicken need a bath? Involving learners in routine animal care can help build routine, care and curiosity

Introducing Children to Animals and Farm Therapy (A Process)

A child-led animal feelings wall is a great way to show and track your observations about the animals. Use children's art, photographs of the animals and the captured observations of animal feelings and behaviours to create a display, or to keep a class journal. To link this to academic outcomes, you could also include growth charts and feed logs to show 'how we care for Hazel' or to showcase the animal's journey from 'nervous to nurturing'.

Assemblies are another great way to share learning and it might help other classes or year groups to hear about moments of calm that children have shared with animals or to join in with a live demonstration of calming techniques that children use with or before their interactions with animals, such as butterfly hugs or box breathing, to help other children to learn about co-regulation, breathing and animal-assisted learning.

While the children you work with directly might benefit from keeping a regular journal (drawn or written) to keep track of their interactions with the animals, if your school has a newsletter or parent update, it might also be nice to include a message from the animal, or an update for children and parents on an 'animal kindness moment of the week' to help share emotional and behavioural gains and reinforce the work happening inside of your classroom.

Involving the rest of the school isn't only a nice way to share your learning, but it also helps to include them in ways that might be beneficial to the sustainability of your project.

There are times that you might need help from the wider school community - what happens, for example, during school holidays or at weekends? Does the animal stay at school or go home with a staff member, or is there a rota of trained families? You may not wish to think about it, but who would be the animal's long-term guardian if the school's circumstances changed? Would a family be able to be part of the rehoming or retirement plan if one was needed? What if you move on or are unwell - could another class provide a home for your animals?

Make it visible for learners throughout your setting when you undertake ongoing training or arrange for updates for staff and animal care team members. This might be training you assemble yourself, or could be something delivered by a local animal charity or vet, but sharing it will help to educate everyone about the benefits of having animals at school, support you in building a network of advocates and volunteers, and raise the profile of your animal provision through showing how invested you are in providing the best environment for the children and the animals that you support.

Allowing your wider school or setting to benefit from animal provision might also allow you to build upon your provision in future, work in collaboration with colleagues (see Emzi's case study in Chapter 6 for some great examples of this) or to apply for funding or other additional budget. How can you support your colleagues to build animal-based learning into their own lesson plans or to grow their understanding of animal-assisted education?

48 Animal-Assisted Learning

We've included some ideas for building a whole-school culture around your animal provision. Using or adapting these ideas should help everyone to benefit, and grow your community support to include learners, colleagues and parents from outside of your core group.

Initiative	Description
'Kindness keeper' badge	Rotating award for students who show gentle, respectful behaviour to animals and peers. Using assemblies or school newsletters to announce a regular recipient of the badge should raise awareness and build interest in the initiative.
Annual Animal Day	A themed day celebrating species knowledge, habitat creation, co-regulation games and storytelling can provide an opportunity for the whole school to learn and develop their animal knowledge together. This could be the culmination of a year of animal-focused interactions (e.g. your wall display) or the basis of the year ahead, setting the scene and providing stimulus for lessons and conversations which 'call back' to the activities of the day.
Whole-School Animal Charter	A co-created policy with input from staff and students, this charter might include 'we promise to' statements and other commitments to animal care, co-regulation and educational aims. Displayed prominently in the animal enclosure, or in a central place within your setting, this charter can help everyone to feel invested in the welfare of the animals and in how their impact is felt across the whole setting.
Staff Training Bank	Create a shared CPD resource folder with information and guidance on co-regulation, animal welfare, trauma-informed animal interventions to help colleagues and contractors to feel safe and supported when planning for, working with and teaching alongside the animals. This could be tactile and paper-based to help colleagues to spend time with the animals or planning offline, or kept online in a central file or on your setting's intranet system, for everyone to access easily.

In this chapter, we've talked about the very beginnings of your project and your first introductions between animals and children. There's a lot to think about, but you've got this! Although we'll help to scaffold your practice with project planning support and through surfacing important considerations, animal-assisted interventions can be intuitive and help make your ongoing planning easier to manage and contextualise.

To support you with planning your project and with breaking things down into manageable tasks that are easy to keep track of, we've developed a checklist of steps and considerations that you might want to use directly in your planning, or to adapt into your own list, contextualised for your setting.

We'll continue to provide lists as we progress through our planning together. Keep them safe and they'll also help you with the assembly of your business case later!

Animal Introductions Checklist

Intention and Planning

- Define learning outcomes: These are your OKRs. Once you've got a 'North Star', everything will be easier to plan and make decisions about.
- Decide on the provision type: Once you know what your goals are, you can decide how best to meet them. Is a full-time animal colleague the best option, or are there other ways that you can start to incorporate animals into your work with learners?
  Remember – a combination of these might meet your requirements best, and it's always possible to build upon your initial plans later. You don't have to go 'all in' when first starting out on your journey.
    - Photo, video or other remote animal interactions
    - Inviting a visiting therapy animal to your setting
    - A short-term project, such as hatching
    - Trip to see animals in an external setting
- Choose species with welfare and logistics in mind – animals' needs are paramount, especially when considering what we know about co-regulation and our need to observe animal behaviour. Unhappy animals are unsafe animals, and a suitable animal will satisfy every one of the points below.
    - A temperament suitable for children, particularly the children in your setting. Animal species each have innate qualities, which will have a bearing on whether they'd be a suitable addition to your setting. Additionally, there are other things to consider when it comes to suitability. Will you buy or adopt your animals, and how might this impact their temperament or the predictability of their behaviour?
    - Safe, predictable and manageable in group settings. Some animals don't like interacting with people, and these are unlikely to be suitable for our needs. Animals that were handled or socialised when they were young, or that are still young, might be more likely to be friendly. Consider the time that the animals might need to recover between sessions and how long they might be expected to 'work' each day. Understanding these boundaries will help to ensure you choose the right animal for your needs.
    - Space and environmental needs considered. You might really want a horse, but even small horses need space, and it's important to provide properly for the animals in your care to keep everyone safe and to model care and empathy through your own interactions with and provision for your animals. Will the animal have access to enough space, light and environmental enrichment to keep them safe and happy? Will the winter temperatures in your classroom be suitable? Consider your setting, the animal's space requirements and how the animal might cope with noise, light and heat.
    - The animal's welfare needs align with the site schedule. You'll need to be able to access the animal's enclosure and provide for their needs, even when the setting is closed. If it's not possible to gain access to your setting during holidays, after hours or through other closures, you'll need to consider animals that can

Copyright material from Phillips and Newman (2026) *Animal-Assisted Learning*, Routledge

come home with you or that visit from elsewhere. Discuss access with your senior team, or your caretaker, before you decide on an animal or move forward in your planning.
- Conduct an initial risk-benefit assessment with parents. This could be through a survey or face-to-face interaction, but it's important to develop a full picture of children's needs and any considerations you might not yet be aware of.
    - Child allergies are surfaced and understood. Do you have children who might need an epi-pen? Might anyone struggle if a furry friend is introduced?
    - You know about children's fears and phobias as they relate to animals and are aware of any sensory issues that might be affected during animal interactions.
    - Health conditions such as immune deficiencies and asthma are disclosed, and you understand how they might be impacted by interactions with your shortlist of animals.
    - You have an understanding of children's previous animal experiences and any cultural beliefs that might influence their animal interactions.
- Gain approvals and consents.
    - At this stage, our first gate is getting approval from site management or facilities teams, to ensure that access can be granted for animal care whenever this is needed. Be clear that access might be required at short notice or by third parties (such as vets) if animals are in distress. Do you need to be a keyholder?

Preparing Children and Staff

- Create and share a social story about the animal: Who are they? Where have they come from? Are they happy to be here? A little scared? Excited? What myths exist about them? What do they want from us?
- Set up introductory materials to help the children to better understand the animal and the behaviours that animals might exhibit (and their own behaviour), and to support the introduction of animals into your practice.
    - Photos, videos, books to help children to better understand the animal.
    - Puppets, animal figures and cuddly animals to help with discussions and modelling good animal interactions.
    - Co-created class rules or animal charter to help children to feel part of the team when it comes to keeping animals safe and well cared for.
    - Visuals for calm-down steps, animal feelings charts and observation cards, and checklists to help to scaffold your teaching and interactions with the animals.
- Plan emotional co-regulation strategies which can help children to both understand and learn techniques for regulating their emotions and reactions when interacting with animals and in their day-to-day.
    - Breathing exercises and active calming activities like butterfly hugs, box breathing and 'legs up the wall' time.
    - Your 'watch and wonder' phase – get out those observation cards and plan all of the ways that children can observe, document and ask questions about the animals. This could be as long a phase as you think would be beneficial and might

widen out into other areas of your practice or curriculum, such as through creative writing exercises and maths interventions.
- Set up a space for children to go if they feel overwhelmed. A calm-down zone or safe space with soft lighting, quiet and access to sensory stimuli, like cuddly animals or fidget toys. It can also be helpful to consider how this space smells, especially if it is within the same space as your animal provision.
- Retreat zone for the animal – same thinking, different unique individual. What does the animal need to feel calm? Is there space for the animal to remove themselves and stay out of sight if they feel overwhelmed or 'on display'? Animals won't be able to work or interact all day and will need a calm and safe space to rest and recover with familiar smells, sounds and enrichment activities.

- Train your colleagues to make sure you have a support network within your setting. Some things that might be helpful to consider are:
  - Reading animal body language – just like your learners, colleagues will need to understand how to assess how animals are feeling and how to use this information to inform the way that they approach interacting with and caring for the animal. Share your observation cards, and challenge colleagues to spend time observing and recording the animals during their breaks or as a way to decompress at the end of the day. Remember that you'll need to be present, at least at first, to help them to learn and stay curious, and to make sure that your animals feel safe.
  - Trauma-informed practice (predictability, consent, no force) can be helpful within animal-assisted education settings, to support both the needs of your learners and the animals. Deploying the same techniques as you might use to help learners to understand co-regulation could be one way to support colleagues' learning about trauma-informed approaches for the first time.
  - Share specific activities and lesson plans that have worked well, which colleagues might like to replicate in their own classrooms. Sharing your own learning and the ideas that work well might inspire others to join your animal project, or help you to spread the impact – maybe colleagues would benefit from running sessions using images, videos and remote interactions with your animals? Could your class share their learning with another?

Environment and Practical Set-Up

- Prepare the space for your chosen animal. You'll need to have spent time understanding what they need and sourcing materials to ensure:
  - The animal enclosure and area is in a quiet, low-traffic location, to allow the animal to rest and recover when they're not playing.
  - There's a designated rest area for the animal, with suitable accommodations for their environmental needs and preferences.
  - You have a seating arrangement for calm observation. Take into account where children might get a good view, feel settled and be safe from animal advances, especially if your chosen animal has the potential to cause harm.

Copyright material from Phillips and Newman (2026) *Animal-Assisted Learning*, Routledge

- Storage for food, cleaning items and enrichment opportunities. Food will need to be protected from the air (and contained in a way that doesn't invite pests), and you'll need space to keep cleaning items (and other potentially dangerous supplies, such as any required animal medications) locked away and safe from children. Enrichment opportunities will vary from animal to animal. Some animals will be easy to buy toys and games for, whereas others might need enrichment through foraging activities, brushes and mirrors, to help stimulate their natural behaviours. Finding the right balance between enrichment and indulgence is also important. Chickens, for instance, will keep themselves occupied by eating treats all day, but this can be detrimental to their health. Adding toys like glockenspiels, climbing equipment and puzzles (which might have hidden treats) can better help to keep chickens entertained without making them ill.

Routine Building and Integration

- Consider developing a daily or weekly rota to help children experience different areas of animal care or interaction. Go back to your objectives again and decide whether children will take turns doing routine animal care tasks and how you'll be able to switch things up when you need to, to accommodate the needs of both your learners and your animals. Will learners need to take turns with animal interactions? Might some days be contact-free? How long will animals be able to interact before needing to rest? Make sure that your rota takes into account:
  - Feeding routines for the animals: Do your animals need to be fed multiple times a day? Are there different stages to feeding (measuring, carrying, feeding, checking) and how will they factor into your rota?
  - Cleaning responsibilities: Who will clean out the animal enclosure? Is this something your learners can help with? Will this happen outside of teaching hours? How often will learners check on animal cleanliness, clean feeding equipment or perform bedding changes?
  - Enrichment planning (e.g. foraging, toy rotation): How will you maintain enrichment for your animals? Just as we lose interest in our toys and home environment, so will they. How often might you need to change around their enclosure or introduce new toys? Will interactions with your learners play part of their enrichment plan? If so, how will you balance rest and play?
- Maintain a reflective journal – for yourself as well as with your learners. While you can put together a journal template to support learners to record their animal observations in text, images or video recordings, it's also possible to create a version for yourself and colleagues, with space to record activities, reflections and ideas for future activities and improvements.
  - Create a student template and a staff version of your reflective journal.
  - Include prompts on learner feelings, animal behaviour, and space for any questions or reflections.

Copyright material from Phillips and Newman (2026) *Animal-Assisted Learning*, Routledge

Whole-School Culture and Celebration

- Share learning and reflections with the rest of your setting, allowing everyone to feel part of your animal experience. This can be done in a number of ways. Spend time considering:
    - Displays
    - Class assemblies
    - Newsletters or blog posts
- Integrate animal-based learning across your curriculum planning to help to embed your learning, normalise the presence of animals in your setting and contextualise and bring to life concepts that might be difficult to understand in theory alone. Return, again, to your objectives. How might you achieve these through incorporating animal interaction? Some ideas and examples include:
    - Literacy: Your learners could develop their literacy skill through writing letters to the animal, or to local animal charities and animal-based organisations, or they might enjoy writing creative stories about their new classmate. For reluctant readers, understanding animal care instructions might be a bigger motivation than reading a book, and if your learners aren't ready for reading or writing, they could practise animal-inspired mark-making or learn about letters and spellings through learning how to say and spell animal names (both the name of the animal species and the animal's own unique name).
    - Science: Animal care is a rich source of opportunities for scientific development. Children can learn about animal life cycles, habitats and behaviour to support their understanding of biology, or you might find it helpful to teach physics concepts such as weight or force through regular feeding interactions or watering. How do the water bottles work in the rabbit hutch? How can a chicken eat from a treadle feeder, but not a mouse? Discussing suitable toys and equipment allows the introduction of concepts like differing states of matter (solids, liquids and gases) and how they might change in different conditions. Why does the lizard's plastic feeder melt when we put it next to the heat lamp? What changes between summer and winter so that we have to go and break ice on top of the outdoor animals' water?
    - Maths: Learners might benefit from using some maths concepts in their day-to-day interactions with animals, such as learning to tell the time through feeding schedules, learning to calculate weight through measuring out food portions, learning to count by observing the number of times an animal completes an action and using differently sized animal water containers to understand shape and volume. Maths concepts taught outside of direct animal interactions can be contextualised for learners using examples from animal care. Using fences or animal housing to aid discussions of angles, or learning 3D shapes through conversations about animal food, toys and enclosures might help learners to picture concepts in real life, increasing both their understanding of the theory in practice and their motivation to learn.

- Create succession and holiday care plans so that your animals are able to be cared for and to mitigate any unexpected failings. What happens if you are unwell or if there's an emergency at school? A good starting point, to consider at this point in our planning, is deciding:
    - Who will care for the animal out of hours/term time?
    - How will they get access?
    - What happens if the animal needs retirement/re-homing?
    - What is your plan for emergencies and animal illnesses?

Keeping the Theory in Mind

Reconnecting to Purpose

Remember earlier, when we talked about how 'calm' might not be the first feeling that springs to mind when you picture a classroom with both excited children and animals? Well, now we've had a look at the theory together and we've started to consider how your project might come together in real life, it's time for us to take a step back to reflect on how you're actually going to make it work in practice. How will you stay true to your values and reap the benefits that you're looking for in your animal provision?

This section will guide you through using your foundational knowledge to stay on course. It will help you to resist the pull of novelty or pressure to prove yourself quickly, and instead keep your focus firmly fixed on your North Star: the objectives that matter most to you and your learners.

Let's return for a moment to the educational theory we explored in Chapters 1 and 2. Remember how we talked about sensory theory, psychological safety and animal-assisted co-regulation? These weren't just nice ideas. The theory is the foundation for every decision you'll make moving forward.

Whether you read it all from beginning to end, furiously taking notes, or you skipped through looking for the ideas that would best fit your own use case, revisiting these principles regularly helps keep your provision learner-centred and ethically sound.

Holding on to Your North Star

There are lots of reminders, in our case studies, that planning must remain responsive and ethical, placing the animal's needs first. Emzi's success at Petroc College (Chapter 6) was only possible because she could explain why every step mattered using evidence-based thinking to back up her instincts and decisions. Keeping the theory in mind isn't about being rigid. It's about being ready to explain, adapt and improve as your setting evolves.

Using OKRs to Stay on Track

In this chapter, we introduced the concept of Objectives and Key Results (OKRs) to help you define what success looks like. Now is a good time to revisit those and make sure they still align with your values, and with the realities of what you've learned through early planning and first encounters.

OKRs work best when they are realistic, measurable and rooted in your setting's specific needs. Consider what will happen when colleagues find out about your animal provision. How easy will it be to protect your provision from 'scope creep' or 'mission creep'?

Scope Creep

Scope creep happens when new tasks, features or goals are added to a project without proper reflection, planning or approval. It often begins with good intentions and can be as simple as hearing yourself say 'Let's just add this one small thing', but scope creep can quickly lead to an overwhelming or unmanageable project.

In animal-assisted education, scope creep might look like:

- Planning a project to bring in a class guinea pig and ending up with a whole school farm before you're fully ready.
- Starting with a goal to improve emotional regulation and then trying to add maths, literacy and science outcomes without support or resources.
- Agreeing to additional sessions or responsibilities that take you away from your original plan or affect the quality of care for your animals.

Mission Creep

Mission creep is a broader concept. It refers to the gradual shift in a project's overarching purpose or intent. It means moving beyond the original mission or values, sometimes without even noticing.

In our context, mission creep might mean:

- Starting with a vision to support vulnerable learners through therapeutic relationships with animals, but slowly becoming more focused on impressing funders, producing data or chasing new audiences at the expense of your core group.
- Moving from a child-led, trauma-informed ethos to a more rigid or results-driven model, because of external pressure to prove your project's success quickly.

In animal-assisted education, both scope creep and mission creep can have serious consequences. They can jeopardise animal welfare by placing too many demands on animals too quickly, without allowing time for proper adjustment or care. The effectiveness of your intervention can become diluted as resources are stretched too thin, leading to inconsistent delivery and reduced impact. Ethical tensions may arise when your work begins to drift away from the values that originally grounded your project, particularly if external pressures push you towards decisions that no longer feel aligned with your intentions. Over time, this relentless expansion can also lead to burnout, for you and your team, as the project begins to outgrow what is realistically sustainable.

In short:

Scope creep adds more tasks.
Mission creep drifts away from your core purpose.

Both can be managed—if you remember why you started.

Remember Why You Started

Returning to your OKRs regularly helps you resist both types of 'creep' and the temptation to chase every exciting opportunity or new idea. Instead, you can evaluate offers and options by asking, 'Will this help me meet my objective?'

Ask yourself regularly:

- Is my objective still the right one?
- Do my key results show progress that really matters to my learners?
- Does the way I'm working with animals support those aims or distract from them?

In a busy teaching role, especially one that involves animal-assisted provision, it can feel like there's little time left for formal reflection. But regular reflection on your OKRs can be something that quietly shapes your thinking, helps you stay true to your values and gives you confidence that your work is making a difference. If you're not good at taking time out for yourself, or to reflect, try to make this a priority. Block out some calendar time and try to treat reflection as a responsibility, rather than a 'nice to have'.

Reflection doesn't have to be heavy-handed, and though we might prefer a spreadsheet with our goals mapped out to track our results, or a notebook and a set of coloured pens so that we can journal our reflections, it might be that you'll work better with a lighter touch. Try prompting yourself with a daily reminder in your calendar or on your to-do list, or if you're more visual, a little laminated card or poster with your main objectives written on it can serve as a daily nudge. It might simply say: 'Are we still on course?' or 'What are we learning today that feeds into our goals?'

Whatever works best for you, try to build the habit of reflection into your daily rhythm as a way to keep your animal-assisted work rooted, meaningful and aligned with what matters most.

4

Risk Assessing Animal Interactions

> Ensuring safety is paramount when integrating animals into education. This chapter discusses risk assessment protocols, from health and safety checks for animals to managing zoonotic disease risks, and provides checklists and guidelines to help educators create a safe learning environment for all involved.

We've already talked in depth about how, if you're considering bringing animals into your classroom or educational setting, you're opening the door to a deeply engaging and emotionally rich learning experience... but why isn't everyone doing it?

You probably wouldn't be reading this book if introducing animals was easy.

There's a lot to think about, and risk assessment is not a box-ticking exercise. When animals are involved, safety becomes more complex, and we're going to need to carry out a thorough, confident and thoughtful risk assessment to make sure that our new animal-assisted learning provision remains magical, supportive and safe.

You might be rolling your eyes at this point. It's unlikely that you've made it this far into your educational career and not had to complete a risk assessment. You could probably share some best practice with us!

But when animals are introduced, the assessment must include human, animal and environmental safety, which is something often outside a teacher's normal remit.

In this chapter, we're going to start at the beginning and work our way through the risk assessment portion of our planning together. If your school uses a specific template or framework for risk assessment, it might be good to keep a copy handy, so that you can adapt this section as you go. We want to make it as easy as possible for the decision maker to say 'yes' to our animal project, and we don't have time to redo our plan if they're in the wrong format.

So... back to basics.

Figure 4.1 Goats can climb and jump so can be hard to contain. This will be important during risk assessment

Starting Your Risk Assessment

What do we mean when we talk about 'doing a risk assessment'? How is it distinct from 'assessing risk'?

A risk assessment is a structured process that helps you to think ahead, identify potential dangers and take the steps needed to reduce (and, in some cases, remove) the likelihood of harm. In an educational context, especially when animals are involved, it's your opportunity to show that you've considered the safety of the children, the welfare of the animals and the suitability of the environment where they'll meet.

Your risk assessment will form a part of your business case, as well as being crucial to keeping everyone safe once you're up and running in your new provision. All of those awkward questions that we're worried that people will ask? We're going to get ahead of 99.9 per cent of them here. In a 2023 podcast for the CACHE Alumni podcast, POD-CACHE, Jenny told Dawn that 'no is just a starting point'. This risk assessment is where we'll find all of the answers that we need to confidently 'argue it out' with the person we're asking for permission from through letting them know that we're ready to make this work.

Put simply, a risk assessment asks:

- What could go wrong? (Hazard)
- Who might be affected, and how? (Potential Harm)

- What are we already doing to prevent this? (Existing Controls)
- What more could we do to reduce the risk further? (Additional Mitigations)

If you prefer to work as you read, grab your risk assessment template or, if you don't have one yet, open a spreadsheet. If you're a 'pen and paper' person, fold a sheet of A4 into half, and then half again so that you have four columns and write these four questions at the top of each.

Hazard	Potential Harm	Existing Controls	Additional Mitigations

Your risk assessment template, whatever its format or branding, is likely to follow a similar structure to this. It will ask similar questions. Take a little time to start thinking within these headers.

Go back to your objectives and start to ask yourself these questions about every idea that pops into your head. You don't need to write anything down yet. Just get your brain working. It might feel a little overwhelming to think about all of the things that could go wrong, so it can be helpful to practise what you preach and go for a walk while you mull things over, or to spend some time with your own pets or animal friends.

Remember - risk assessment isn't about eliminating all risk (which is impossible), but about thoughtful planning. It's about showing that you understand the risks involved and have put reasonable, proportionate measures in place to keep everyone as safe as possible, including yourself, the children and the animals.

A Chance to Reflect

Ideally, your own wellbeing will be included in the risk assessment. It's something that you're almost certain to neglect to properly consider, but it's incredibly important. According to the National Educational Union (2025), approximately nine in ten teachers experience work-related stress at least 20 per cent of the time, and around 62 per cent feel stressed more than 60 per cent of the time. Younger and female teachers, especially in early years and primary phases, report higher stress levels. Seventy-five per cent say they struggle to switch off from work at home, and many regularly work evenings and weekends.

How will adding animal care and wellbeing to your workload be managed? What are the risks to you and your wellbeing, and how can you negate them?

Let's use this question as an example risk for our planning. We'll need to explore it in more detail before we write it up in our risk assessment format.

Introducing animals into the classroom can have a complex impact on teacher stress. It can ease stress in some areas, but also introduce new pressures. Whether the effect is positive or negative often depends on how well the animal provision is planned, resourced and supported.

The presence of animals can shift the emotional tone of the classroom, creating a calmer and more nurturing atmosphere. Animals are known to reduce anxiety and heart rate in humans, and this effect isn't limited to children. It seems obvious that teachers can benefit too. When the classroom feels calmer, behaviour improves and relationships strengthen, the daily pressures might feel easier to navigate.

Animals can support teacher wellbeing by reintroducing joy, curiosity and connection into the day. In emotionally demanding roles, particularly when supporting children with complex needs, animals can serve as co-regulators and offer moments of softness, humour or warmth that make the day feel more manageable.

But it's important to acknowledge that animals can also increase stress, especially if the responsibility for their care falls solely on the teacher, adding to an already full workload. Without a clear plan for cleaning, feeding and cover during weekends or holidays, what starts as an idea to increase joy and ease tension can quickly become burdensome. If teachers feel unprepared or lack confidence in handling animals safely, or if the needs of the

Figure 4.2 Animal care can add new complexity to balancing practitioner wellbeing

animal aren't fully understood, ethical and welfare concerns may also arise. This can be particularly stressful when safeguarding or health and safety risks haven't been clearly addressed, leaving teachers feeling exposed or unsupported. Even the simple presence of an animal can be a source of strain if not everyone in the setting is on board. For a teacher already managing complex behaviour, special educational needs or heavy workload, being asked to also care for a living creature and meaningfully integrate that into their teaching day can feel overwhelming.

Putting It All Together

So, we know what the problem is now. We've got an idea of what might go wrong and, at this stage, it might seem like a lot. Don't let the weight of the risk worry you. We need to break it down and properly consider the mitigations before we decide whether this risk is as big as it seems.

Let's do that now.

Splitting this risk out into its constituent parts will help us to better understand it, and to manage it. It's unlikely that one change would mitigate every part of this risk, so let's look at it in smaller chunks.

What Are the Hazards?

In our hazards column, we can list out the potential hazards in this scenario. There's the increased teacher workload and emotional stress due to responsibility for animal care and management, and because it might also impact on your wellbeing, there's also the potential hazard that unclear boundaries around animal interaction might lead to conflict or confusion among colleagues.

Write these down as two separate hazards in your risk log. If you're working on paper, don't forget to take them one at a time so that you don't run out of space for mitigations!

Think about the potential harm from the hazards, one by one.

For the first hazard, about your increased workload, the potential for harm might be emotional strain, the risk of burnout or increased anxiety due to feeling overwhelmed by added responsibilities. Guilt or concern might be felt if animal welfare is perceived as compromised. You may experience frustration if expectations are unclear or unsupported. Disruption to working patterns, particularly outside school hours (e.g. holidays, weekends), might impact on your work-life balance.

In hazard number two, where we're considering the risk to your wellbeing arising from disagreements with colleagues about animal care or even just their presence, the potential for harm might come from tension within the staff team if expectations are not communicated well. Some staff might feel uncomfortable around animals, or there could be disagreement about animal access to shared spaces.

Now that we've broken the overall risk down into the hazards and considered the potential harms that might arise, it might already feel a little bit lighter. The clearer the risks are, the easier they are to mitigate and manage... so let's go on to consider that next.

Adding Controls

What already exists in your setting to help you to mitigate these risks?

Let's continue in the format of our form and consider the first hazard first.

List out the existing support in place. Do you have access to CPD or training about animal-assisted learning? Are there opportunities for regular check-ins to monitor staff wellbeing? Would you have the option to pause or adapt provision if staff capacity changes? These are our existing controls. We can mark these down in our risk assessment.

While we're thinking about the first hazard, let's also consider the possible mitigations. What could you introduce, or could your setting introduce, to further reduce the risk of harm?

Could you put a written animal care plan into place, with clear daily and out-of-hours responsibilities? Will you be able to allocate care responsibilities across a number of staff members or nominate a designated animal welfare lead? Might you seek external support or find an advisor to help troubleshoot issues related to animal behaviour or care? This might be a good time to consider opportunities for building supportive partnerships with animal organisations in your local area.

You might feel better after writing out your potential mitigations... or you might be right back to feeling a little overwhelmed. More stuff to do! Try to remember that risk assessment is about planning. We'll unpick all of this work as we go on. It's so much easier to negate risk when we have a plan ready!

For hazard number two, where we worried about potential conflict, the existing controls might see some crossover with our first hazard. Those opportunities for regular check-ins might be helpful if things get heated, and training about animal-assisted learning might help colleagues to better understand, or support, your provision. Additionally, there might be some obvious opportunities for staff to opt out of direct contact with the animal provision.

For your potential mitigations, you might be hoping to agree guidance on where and when animals are present, and to consult with colleagues before going ahead with any animal-assisted project. What are your plans for making sure you have transparent communication with all stakeholders, including midday supervisors, site and support staff?

Reviewing Risk Levels

We've done a lot so far. We've considered a risk, broken it down into hazards, identified the potential harms and listed the existing and potential controls that will allow us to better mitigate that risk. From here, it could be tempting to start to make plans and move forward.

But first, let's go back to the original risk.

When we first considered the risk to our wellbeing, it felt a little bit heavy. It might even have felt like too much to consider. We've probably all encountered risks during our planning that have made us consider giving up on our whole idea, but, often, breaking risks down allows us to find ways to mitigate, reduce or even remove them.

Reconsider each hazard in your list. Once you apply the controls, existing or potential, how much risk is there? Can you find controls that will reduce your risk to low or medium? Note down the residual risk after your controls are in place and write what these rely on.

Our current two hazards, if all of the controls were applied, might now be classified as low to medium risk. This would depend on staffing levels, clarity of roles and how well the needs of the teacher and animal are matched to the school environment.

We've got a lot more risks to get through, but a lot of them will be much less complex than this one... and 'washing our hands after every interaction' is a control that will apply to more of them than you might think.

Just as in the classroom, it's impossible to plan for every risk. People and animals are both unpredictable, to some degree. That's why you do what you do!

To begin with, ask yourself what kind of interactions you're planning. Will children be observing animals from a distance? Will they be feeding, grooming, cleaning out or engaging in more direct forms of animal care? Each type of contact carries its own set of considerations. You'll want to take into account not just the safety of the children but also the physical and emotional wellbeing of the animals. The risks involved for both animals and children are very different if you're talking about a goat being stroked for five minutes or one being led around a field by a group of overexcited seven-year-olds.

Think through each interaction separately, and for each potential hazard that you identify, consider the controls and the residual risk. What might happen? How can you reduce the chances of harm?

Think about your children. You'll want to take a moment to reflect on their individual needs. Does a child have a sensory processing difficulty that might make them respond unpredictably to certain sounds or textures? Is there a child in your group who is non-speaking and might find it hard to express if they're scared or overwhelmed? Tailoring your risk assessment to include these needs is not only good practice, but it can also strengthen the case for your project by showing that it is inclusive, well thought out and rooted in the real needs of your learners.

All of the risks that we've talked about so far have been human-specific. Of course, many of the biggest risks in any animal-assisted setting will involve the animals themselves, but the main hazard isn't animal aggression, as you might first consider, but misunderstanding.

Go back to your objectives and think about your activities through that lens. What is it that might go wrong?

Children might not recognise the signs that an animal is becoming overstimulated or needs space. Animals, particularly prey animals like rabbits or sheep, may feel cornered and stressed in noisy or unfamiliar environments. Including a section in your risk assessment that details how you will monitor animal welfare, including checking body language, offering retreat spaces and limiting interaction times, is essential. This shows that your approach is not only child-safe but also ethical and compassionate. And when thinking about your animal introductions earlier, you've already considered a lot of this.

Think too about the environment. You've already got a good idea of which animal species might best support your aims, and you know about what they need, where they'll live and how they like things to be. Are you using a classroom? An outdoor paddock? A mobile animal experience visiting the school grounds? What are the hygiene facilities like? Do you have appropriate access to handwashing and signage? Will there be enough adults present to supervise safely, and are they trained or briefed in how to respond if something unexpected happens?

Depending on your answers to these questions, you'll have some great existing controls and a good start on a list of potential mitigations that you can use when considering your activities and their associated hazards.

Filling in the Blanks

Your setting might have conducted risk assessments for other, similar activities, and you might find it helpful to look at existing examples of risk assessments for gardening, cooking or farm visits. These often highlight familiar hazards such as tools being used improperly, slips and trips, water hazards and exposure to germs like *E. coli*, which is a particular hazard with many animal interactions. The templates aren't there to be copied word for word, but to give you a solid foundation and show you examples of risk assessment and mitigation in your own context. Your final, well-written animal risk assessment will possibly echo many of the same themes that you see in these previous examples, like sensible supervision, clear instructions and good hygiene, but will also include the more nuanced consideration of animal behaviour and interaction.

Considering both your objectives and your chosen animal assistant, you'll need to carry out some specific research. Are there any risks associated with your animal that you might not have anticipated? In sheep, several infections that can cause abortion in ewes are also dangerous to human pregnancies, meaning you'll need specific controls to protect any colleagues or visitors who might be at risk, especially in spring, when lambing typically occurs. Rabbits can carry zoonotic diseases such as *salmonella*, ringworm and pasteurellosis, with the risk being reduced through the practice of good hygiene when handling and housing your rabbits. Other common therapy animals like dogs are often viewed as 'low risk' because of their familiarity, but they also bring their own specific concerns. Fleas and mites can spread to children or other animals, and dogs that are raw-fed or have access to animal carcasses may carry roundworm, which can be transmitted through faeces and may cause serious illness in humans, particularly children.

Incorporating Feedback

Once you've considered the big and small risks, and your first draft is complete, get a fresh pair of eyes on it. It might seem scary to share it with someone in your school, or with someone who knows the local procedures or has done something similar in their setting, but their feedback might help you to pick up on small details you've missed or give you the reassurance that you're on the right track.

If sharing the full document is too much to consider, or you're worried about confidentiality, consider asking someone you trust to talk things through with you. Tell them what you're planning and ask them to play the part of the gatekeeper or decision maker. They should try to ask you any question, concern or objection that they can think of, and using your risk assessment, you should be able to answer.

If you find that there are questions that you can't answer, you might have discovered a new hazard, and at that point, you know what to do. Head back to your risk assessment and consider this one too!

This is good practice, and it's important to remember that a risk assessment isn't static. It should be reviewed, updated and adjusted every time to find a new risk or hazard. If your animals change, or your group of children changes, so too should your assessment. And that's a good thing. It shows you're responding in real time to the needs of your setting, your children and your stakeholders, and treating the work of bringing animals into education with the seriousness and respect that it deserves.

Thinking Through the Risks Checklist

- Use a structured format: When documenting your risks, work with the four headings: *Hazard, Potential Harm, Existing Controls, Additional Mitigations*. You can fold an A4 sheet or use your school's risk template.
- Identify the types of interaction: What will children be doing with or near the animal? Observation, handling, grooming, feeding or cleaning? Consider how each activity presents unique risks.
- Define your environment: Are interactions taking place indoors or outside? In a dedicated animal room, classroom corner, or temporary setup? The setting impacts supervision, movement, and safety.
- Consider individual needs: Take note of any child-specific risks – allergies, phobias, sensory sensitivities, communication needs or medical vulnerabilities. Think about how you'll manage these inclusively.
- Assess animal needs and behaviour: Consider species-specific behaviours, known risks (e.g. zoonotic infections) and the individual temperament of the animal. How do they show when they are tired or stressed? Could this lead to harm?
- Break down your risks: List potential hazards clearly – for example, scratches or bites, zoonotic transmission, unpredictable child behaviour, stress or injury to the animal, emotional overload for staff.
- Link risks to potential harm: Who could be affected, and how? Include children, staff, volunteers, animals, visiting professionals or families. Don't forget to consider your own wellbeing.
- Note your existing controls: These might include adult supervision, trained handlers, restricted access, pre-session briefings or hygiene policies already in place.
- Brainstorm further mitigations: Could you stagger groups, reduce session length or add visual cues for children and staff? Could you schedule rest days or reduce handling time?
- Assess residual risk: After applying controls, ask: What level of risk remains? Low, medium, or high? Is this level acceptable in your setting?
- Share and discuss: Talk your assessment through with a trusted colleague or senior leader. Ask them to challenge your thinking. Their feedback might strengthen your case.

Copyright material from Phillips and Newman (2026) *Animal-Assisted Learning*, Routledge

Setting Up for Safety Checklist

- Install a handwashing station: Ensure this is easily accessible and signposted, and includes soap, warm water and disposable towels. If not possible, have alcohol-free hand gel and wipes available, and consider carefully whether this is suitable for the needs of your children and your animals. Without handwashing facilities, are you introducing risks that are insurmountable?
- Provide PPE where appropriate: You might wish to make gloves available for any feeding, cleaning, or health-related animal tasks, or need hearing or eye protection for your learners. Try to store them nearby, clearly labelled and in the right size for children and adults, so that people can help themselves.
- Use pet-safe cleaning supplies: Bleaches and harsh chemicals can harm animals, and some disinfectants just won't work on zoonotic diseases or viruses. Use proper cleaning products for your situation, which are approved for use around animals, and store them safely out of reach of children.
- Put up clear visual signage: Create 'Animal Area' signs and floor markers that help children to recognise boundaries. Picture-based symbols can be especially useful for non-reading or younger learners. Are you ready to involve your children in the preparations? If so, getting them to make signage might be a great opportunity to introduce discussions about animal welfare, co-regulation needs and how you'll all make it work.
- Consider the use of Green/Amber/Red zones: Coded zones might be helpful while the children learn to read animal behaviour cues for themselves. These are colourful signs or visual cues which show the animal's current readiness to interact. Green = ready, Amber = observe only, Red = no contact. They can be used to help learners to understand how animals might feel and to provide immediate and clear boundaries.
- Think about retreat zones: Both children and animals need safe spaces to decompress, especially when everything is so exciting! Animals should have a quiet, private area they can access freely at all times, and children may need a sensory calm space nearby.

Avoiding Burnout Checklist

- Include staff wellbeing in your risk planning: What happens if you're unwell or overwhelmed? Who covers animal care? How will you manage extra workload and still get rest? An important question to ask yourself before you make any firm decisions is: Who's going to do this on Christmas Day/my birthday/when I'm on holiday?
- Name your support network: Who is your 'animal backup'? Who can feed, clean or monitor the animal in your absence or during out-of-hours? Document this clearly and try to stick to your plans. If you do find that you're doing more of the work than you anticipated, address it early. Remember – scope creep takes us away from our mission.
- Keep wellbeing in check for the animals too: Monitor for signs of stress, overstimulation or illness. Keep a basic welfare log if animals are present regularly. Unwell animals place additional pressure on you to prioritise the animals. It's always better to seek help early if you're unsure. Do you have a vet available if you need one? How will expenses work in an emergency? Make sure to seek answers to these questions as part of your planning.
- Think about noise, movement and volume: Lots of animals are sensitive to unpredictable movement or loud sound. Could you introduce 'quiet time' cues or embed this into your classroom routine? Do your animals need a space that's in a different part of the building? How will you regulate for their needs?

5

The Boring Stuff

Business Casing, Planning and Overcoming Objections in an Educational Setting

> Alongside risk assessment, the administrative and strategic planning aspects of implementing an animal-based project are crucial for sustainability. Here, we cover how to make a compelling business case for animal-assisted education, navigate school and local authority policies, secure funding and address common objections from stakeholders, ensuring that programmes not only start but thrive.

What Is a Business Case?

We've already thought in depth about what we want to achieve and what we might need to make it happen, but to go any further, we're likely to need a business case. It might be frustrating to deal with the paperwork side of setting up your project, but a business case can be great support and helps us to provide a good structure to our arguments for the project, as well as outlining how we're going to achieve our objectives and key results.

A business case is a structured proposal that outlines the rationale for undertaking a project or initiative. It explains *what* the project is, *why* it's needed, *how* it will be done, *who* will do it and *what* the expected benefits are. Think of it as a persuasive document or conversation aimed at decision makers to secure their official approval, investment or support. Like the risk assessment, it might sound official and scary at first, but we've already done a lot of the work in setting our objectives, defining our key results and completing our risk assessment. All of these things will come together, as we work together in this chapter, to help you to build a strong business case.

Imagine that you're trying to convince a friend to go on holiday somewhere new. You'd probably tell them where you're going, why it's worth the time and money, what you'll do there, how much it costs and what you'll get out of it (fun, rest and adventure), alongside doing a brief risk assessment. A business case is the same, but for our working wants.

You'll find lots of schools of thought on business cases, and some are, admittedly, quite cumbersome and heavy. We're going to use an agile approach to building our business case. That means we'll keep it flexible, focused on outcomes and open to change. The most effective business cases aren't necessarily the longest, and a lot of the detail already exists in our risk assessment. Together, we're going to build a business case where we can communicate value, demonstrate care and respond to the needs of everyone involved – children, animals and colleagues alike.

The Principles of a Business Case

Just like your animal provision, and the planning that we've done so far, your business case should feel alive. This document will be something that grows and evolves as your understanding deepens and your stakeholders get involved. It's a 'living document' and we can make changes any time we get new information, or when something changes.

We'll anchor our case in four key principles:

1. Delivering Value Quickly

Your proposal should show how this project will make a positive difference straight away. Remember how we talked about starting small and building as you gain confidence and find your sea legs? Think about what changes you could observe within weeks. Are you expecting to see reduced anxiety in your learners? Increased engagement in maths lessons? A disconnected class that starts to feel more like a team?

2. Iterative Learning

You don't need to have everything mapped out from the beginning to run a successful project. Instead, build just enough case to get started and then adapt as you go. We've done an extensive risk assessment and we know what the landscape around us looks like, how we plan to navigate it and what might go wrong. Learning happens in real time, and your business case should reflect that.

3. Learner-Centred Outcomes

Your business case should advocate for the needs of your learners and clearly show how the project benefits the children, with the same warmth and attentiveness you'd use when advocating for them one-to-one. Your written business case doesn't have to feel formal or stuffy. Let the person reading it feel the care and support that you're putting in place through your planning and reflection.

4. Flexible Funding

Rather than asking for everything that you might need upfront, consider how you'll manage costs over time and explain the longer-term commitment to your decision maker in your business case. What do you need right now? What will you need if things go well? Breaking your funding request into phases makes it easy for your setting to support you incrementally, as benefits become visible.

Scoring Your Case – Before You Submit

Before you share your business case, you might want to do a little reflective check-in using the scorecard below. It's a gentle way to self-assess how strong your case is, and where you might want to firm it up. Give each category a score out of 5 and add them together to get a final score.

Rough Business Case Scorecard

Category	Questions to Ask	Score
Educational Value	Does the animal support specific curriculum goals like science, empathy or communication?	
Student Engagement	Will this improve motivation, attendance or emotional regulation?	
Operational Feasibility	Does care seem manageable during school days and holidays?	
Cost Management	Are costs clear and realistic? Do you have a funding plan?	
Risk and Compliance	Have you anticipated and planned for risks?	
Community Buy-In	Are parents, staff and children supportive? Have you gathered their views or covered how you propose to?	
Sustainability	Will this still work a year from now? Can it be adapted or scaled?	
Total Score:		**/ 35**

You can use this to assess your case before presenting it. Low scores highlight where to strengthen your proposal before you submit it for consideration.

How to Use Objections

Objections are golden opportunities. Although it can feel like negativity, finding out what people have concerns about within your proposal is a great chance to make improvements and benefit from the expertise of the people providing you with feedback. Objections can seem intimidating or off-putting, but it's important to keep a positive mindset and reflect on the reasons that someone has given for objecting. Try not to be defensive, and consider how you can answer their objection with a response that will change their mind. Objections are usually signs that someone cares enough to want to understand more. Think of each objection as an opportunity to strengthen your case and see your project from another angle.

Business Casing, Planning and Overcoming Objections 73

Try responding to objections like this:

Objection	Suggested Response
'Who'll look after it?'	Share your rota and backup plan, and include holiday cover. Invite collaboration with colleagues and parent volunteers.
'What about allergies?'	Choose low-allergen animals, and share your allergy risk assessment early.
'What if it dies?'	Acknowledge this with sensitivity and show how it could support grief education.
'Isn't it distracting?'	Share evidence, or a pilot outcome, showing improvements in regulation and focus.
'Where is the funding coming from?'	List your budget sources and make the case for long-term sustainability or short-term trial.

Each concern should appear in the risk assessment section of your business case, if you haven't already got them recorded.

Figure 5.1 Planning and risk assessing your provision will help to keep everyone safe... even from each other

Building Your Business Case

Just like our risk assessment, the building of the business case can feel a little bit intimidating when we first start to think about it. You might even be thinking, 'Woah, hang on. We're talking about handing this giant document in and working with objections and I haven't even started yet.' And that's OK. We're going to look at this together, step by step.

And again, as with our risk assessment, your setting might work with a specific business case template, and that's also OK. If they do, grab yourself a copy and get familiar with it. You'll need to think about where each of these sections translates to your template and transpose what we do together to the right place on your copy. Even if your setting doesn't have a template of its own, you might prefer to play with the format of this example, to adapt things as you build your case, and that's absolutely OK. Remember, through this whole process we're going to remain flexible, focused on outcomes and open to change.

A.   Executive Summary

Our executive summary introduces our project in the simplest and most effective way that we can. It's usually only one or two strong paragraphs, which state what you're proposing and why.

> We propose introducing a classroom pet to enhance emotional wellbeing, foster responsibility and improve engagement in learning. Our proposal is designed to be safe, ethical and sustainable, with strong links to curriculum and pastoral goals.

You'll need to revisit your objectives and key results for this. What are you trying to achieve and how are you proposing to get there? We'll list out our OKRs in the next section, but this opening paragraph or two gives us the opportunity to start strong with setting out the benefits.

B.   Objectives

List out your Objectives and Key Results (OKRs) clearly in this section. You've already got these nicely formatted, with your objectives clearly supported and measurable using your key results. There's nothing left to do here. Add them into this section and let them shine.

C.   Benefits

Think about your listed OKRs and consider what the benefits of them are.

For example, our OKR example from earlier was;

Objective: Foster stronger peer cooperation skills among students during animal care routines.

Key result 1: 80 per cent of participating students demonstrate improved cooperation skills as observed during animal care activities by the end of term.
Key result 2: At least three peer-led animal care tasks are successfully completed each week without adult intervention.
Key result 3: 90 per cent of students receive positive peer feedback on cooperation at least once during the term.
Key result 4: Incidents of peer conflict during animal care routines are reduced by 50 per cent compared to the start of term.

If we achieve this objective, measured by the key results, it could have far-reaching benefits, not just during the specific activities but throughout the whole of a child's classroom and school life.

Shared responsibility for animals naturally encourages teamwork. When learners have to rely on each other to complete real, meaningful tasks like feeding, cleaning or observing the animals for a project, they learn to communicate clearly, share responsibilities fairly and negotiate roles with empathy. These are vital interpersonal skills that might translate into more cohesive group work, calmer transitions and improved classroom dynamics more broadly.

Additionally, if 80 per cent of learners show improved cooperation, that suggests that you might be seeing evidence of a shift towards a more collaborative culture in which children are not only more willing to work together, but also more able to recognise the needs and contributions of their peers. This improved collaboration can reduce teacher workload over time, as children begin to support each other and resolve minor disagreements without adult intervention, and could help to improve the confidence and inclusion of children who may not otherwise thrive in traditional peer settings. Children who find it easier to communicate or engage when the focus is on an animal, rather than on themselves, might begin to find it easier to feel like part of the group.

When the children complete peer-led tasks independently, they begin to see themselves as capable, trusted members of the school community. This kind of autonomy can boost self-esteem and help children to better learn expectations around responsibility and mutual respect. Similarly, receiving positive feedback from peers not only strengthens relationships, but helps children build a positive sense of belonging and pride, further adding to the collaborative classroom culture.

And importantly, if incidents of peer conflict reduce significantly during animal care routines, it could be an indicator that children are learning to self-regulate, compromise and consider perspectives beyond their own. In a wider school context, this could lead to a calmer atmosphere during other high-pressure or unstructured times of day, such as playtimes or transitions, with children carrying their cooperative behaviours into other parts of school life.

76   Animal-Assisted Learning

When you write out your benefits, try to give them a title or header, to make them very clear, but also, as we have above, frame these from multiple angles so that you can show that you've considered the benefits for the children (emotional regulation, social connection), the curriculum (science, literacy) and your classroom dynamics (teamwork, co-regulation, empathy).

Depending on how you find it easiest, you could segment this by addressing each recipient in turn (children, curriculum and classroom) and listing out the benefits for each, or you could take each OKR in turn, considering the impact on each area.

Once you've brought your OKRs to life with some reflection on the benefits, consider which benefits might be attained outside of your OKRs. There might be additional benefits that you won't be actively working on, but which will reveal themselves through your other focus areas.

Remember that your OKRs are measurable and tangible. This is a different section, where you can flesh out your OKRs with additional benefits and add colour and context to your goals. Not everything has to be measurable to the same degree as your Key Results do, but you will need to consider how you'll know if the benefits take root, even if it's a light-touch measurement like 'things will feel less tense'.

D.   Options Considered

This section of a business case can be tempting to exclude. It can be an understandable concern that you'll detract from your case by presenting alternative solutions, but it's important to show that you've been open to alternatives and have fully explored them before making your recommendation. and it's a great way to show why your recommended option is the best choice!

In this section of your business case, you should talk about each of your options in turn and explain the pros and cons of each. Clearly explain why your preferred option is the one that you recommend and try to anticipate any questions that you might need to answer about the suitability of the options you've excluded.

Remember, our options included the option of a full-time provision with an animal coming to live in your setting full-time, a visiting animal, a trip out to see animals elsewhere, or no direct animal provision. Don't forget to include no provision as an option. We want to show why this option carries risk and why our chosen option is the preferred solution.

As an example, with no context from your setting, these four options might look something like:

Option 1: Full-Time Animal Provision (Recommended Option)

This option would see a suitable animal (or animals) come to live in the setting on a full-time basis, becoming a consistent part of the school community and providing daily opportunities for structured and informal learning.

Pros

This option provides the greatest potential for sustained impact. With daily access, children can build ongoing relationships with the animals, develop routines and responsibilities, and engage in regular cooperative tasks. This approach allows animal care to become embedded in the rhythm of school life, would support emotional regulation and peer cooperation, and help to provide a calm, relational learning environment. Having a full-time animal also enables a greater degree of flexibility and integration with the curriculum and therapeutic support. It supports deep learning over time and allows staff to plan for progressive development in both practical skills and social-emotional learning.

Cons

This approach requires a significant commitment of time, resources and planning. There are practical considerations around housing, staffing, weekends/holidays and veterinary care. However, these are mitigated through good planning, clear protocols and sharing responsibility across staff. Importantly, the benefits of sustained relationship building and impact on school culture far outweigh these challenges.

Option 2: Visiting Animal Provision

In this model, external providers visit the school at regular or one-off intervals, bringing animals for short, supervised interactions or sessions.

Pros

This option benefits from a lower upfront commitment and risk. There is no need for on site housing or full-time care, and activities can be run by trained external staff. Good for schools trialling animal work or with limited space or resources.

Cons

The impact possible with this approach is limited by the short duration and infrequency of visits. There's little opportunity for deep relationship building with the animals and the novelty factor of the visit may fade quickly without integration into wider provision. It can also be more difficult to align visits with specific learning or behaviour goals without working with the visiting organisation on a bigger project, and is innately reliant on external timetables, reducing the flexibility of timetabling for this interaction.

Option 3: Off-Site Animal Visits/Trips

This option involves taking students out of the school environment to visit farms, sanctuaries or education centres where animals are kept by external organisations.

Pros

With this approach, children stand to benefit from high-welfare animal environments and immersive learning experiences, with no pressure on the school to provide care facilities or natural habitats for animals. This could be beneficial for linking to specific curriculum areas, such as 'the natural world' or for learners who may benefit from change of scene.

Cons

These sorts of trips are usually infrequent, require additional funding and risk assessment, and are often only accessible to a limited number of students. There's a requirement for additional chaperones to support our learners when off-site, and although the impact can be powerful, it tends to be short-lived. These trips do not support routine or day-to-day development of cooperation and responsibility in the same way as on-site provision might.

Option 4: No Direct Animal Provision

This option is to continue with our current provision and not introduce animal-assisted activity at this time.

Pros

No additional cost, risk or planning required. Avoids need for any changes to site or policy.

Cons

This option fails to address the identified need for developing cooperation and peer relationships through shared, meaningful tasks. It misses the opportunity to introduce a powerful, relationship-centred learning tool and may result in continued barriers to engagement for some students. Not acting also means falling behind other settings trialling animal-assisted interventions, and could limit the school's ability to innovate or adapt to pupil needs in creative ways.

After you have outlined all four options, contextualised for your setting and learners, it's usually a good idea to reiterate your preferred option, with any additional rationale, like this:

> **Recommendation: Option 1 – Full-Time Animal Provision**
>
> Of the options explored, full-time animal provision offers the most comprehensive and sustainable means of achieving our objectives. It has great potential to support our routine and to deepen the relationships we have with learners and also those that they have with each other. This provision could become a living part of school culture,

which is something that children can contribute to, take pride in and learn from every day. While this option does require planning and commitment, the potential return in terms of emotional growth, cooperation skills and community cohesion is significant. By selecting this option, we would be investing in something that will not only support the children now, but will continue to shape a compassionate, inclusive and relational school environment for years to come.

E. Costs and Financial Plan

Split your budget into set-up and ongoing costs. Be honest, not ambitious. Asking for more than you need, at this point, won't win us any advocates. Realistic asks build trust.

Equally, asking for too little will also invite failure. Running out of money is a risk. Offer flexibility in how funding might be staged or shared, but don't underestimate how much you'll need to make things work.

Just as asking for feedback is a way to invite people into your project and get them on board, being clear about your financial planning is a great way to show that you're professional. Showing your working out and being clear about your needs also invites people to offer help. Make it clear what you need, and it should be much easier for people to tell you what they can give.

The key here is to keep it as simple as you can. Your sample budget might look something like this:

Expense	Cost
Habitat set-up (one time)	£30–£70
Animal purchase (one time)	£30 per guinea pig (£30 x 3) = £90
Food (monthly)	£5–£10 (£10 x 12) = £120
Bedding (monthly)	£5 (£5 x 12) = £60
Vet contingency	£50/year
Toys/Extras	£30/year
First year total	£70 + £90 + £120 + £60 + £50 + £30 = £420

Do your research and complete each section with your real estimates.

Pair this with a clear explanation of how you'll cover costs: school funds, funding bids, class fundraisers, community donations or charity grant schemes and local funds.

Small pots of money are often easier to find than you think!

80   Animal-Assisted Learning

> Many local councils offer small grants for community or educational projects, especially those linked to wellbeing, outdoor learning or inclusion. Check your local authority's website or contact their education or community engagement team. Community foundations (regional charities that distribute grants on behalf of donors) are also worth investigating as they often have rolling or seasonal funds that support schools and youth projects. National charities and trusts often fund projects that promote mental health, social connection, environmental awareness or SEND support – look into funding from the National Lottery, Children in Need and the Co-op's Community Fund.

These funds will usually ask for a short proposal and a breakdown of how you'll spend the money, so spending this time on getting your business case right means we can use it as a supportive document again and again.

Although you won't need to include all of this information in your business case, knowing what funding is available, and how you might access it, will help you to project where you think the money for your project might come from.

Figure 5.2 Could working with local charities help to add support or reduce costs?

Once you've got a list of your projected costs and an outline of where you think the money will come from, you can write these into your business case and move on.

F. Risks and Mitigations

Include your risk assessment here. You can include the whole assessment in this section, or summarise the key risks, controls and mitigations in paragraph form, and include the full assessment as an appendix. Either way, you should be starting to see how far we already are in building our case. We've already done a lot of the work in putting things together.

Now is a good time to review your risk assessment again. Has your business case raised risks you hadn't previously included? What about your budgeting task? Is there a risk you'll run out of money? That funding won't come through? Now's the time to jot it down here, along with your controls and mitigations.

And that's it for this section!

G. Project Plan

In this section, we're going to think about the plans we made earlier. How will we build enclosures, house our animals and introduce our learners to both the new environment they'll be learning in and their new classroom colleagues? Map out the journey to 'ideal' from where you are now and show your planning week by week, making it easy to follow and easy to say yes to.

This might be an exciting activity, as you start to see your project become more tangible, but it can also be confusing, especially if you've never done it before.

But there's a lot of crossover between a business case and a project plan, especially in the early stages of turning an idea into something that can be supported and resourced… so we've already done a lot of the work here!

A business case often explains why your option is the best choice. In your project plan, take that same logic and shape it into steps. For example:

> Business case:
> 'Full-time provision allows for sustained, meaningful relationships between pupils and animals, supporting regulation and cooperative skills.'
>
> Project plan:
> 'We will introduce a classroom rabbit from October onwards. Daily care routines will be scheduled into morning group tasks. A weekly rota will be developed with pupils and supported by staff. This will be trialled for one term.'

Take your recommendations and turn them into a rough calendar. Even a very simple timeline (e.g. 'September: prepare housing and staff training', 'October: introduce animal', 'November: begin pupil rota') helps keep everyone on the same page. You might want to keep a simple table or checklist to track what's been done and what's next. The ones we've provided should help you to think about what you might want to include in your tracker.

Keep it simple and don't worry about not having all the answers yet. Some of your actions will be dependent on the outcome of others. Our project plan should be a high-level plan right now, ready for us to add to and reshape later. A well-thought-out business case is a solid foundation, and the process of turning it into a project plan is just about moving from *why we should do this* to *how we're going to do it*.

Give your decision maker enough information so that they can picture what your project might look like, but don't make it too complicated.

H. Conclusion and Call to Action

This is another area of business casing that can be neglected, but it's a really important one. After outlining your objectives, showing how you'll reach them and demonstrating that you've considered how to solve problems as they arise, you'll need to remind the decision maker who reads your business case of what this project could unlock and ask for the specific thing you need. Whether that's funding, permission or time to trial, this is your perfect opportunity to ask for it specifically and tell them again why it's important, or what the risks are of doing nothing.

To complete your business case and reflect all the hard work that you've done in the quality of your conclusion, you'll want to include another short summary of your recommendation, a final summary of what the benefits are and a prompt for action.

Reaffirm what the project will help you achieve. Focus on the real, meaningful impact that the project has the opportunity to provide for learners. This is where you bring the heart of your case back to the surface: how will children grow, feel, learn or connect differently because of this work, and how can your decision maker help you to achieve it?

Once your business case is approved, it becomes your roadmap, so all this work is going to be worth it as we keep moving. Check in with your business case regularly, once you get the go-ahead. Update it when things shift, and don't forget to celebrate the small wins.

6
Farm School Is Open! Now What?

> This chapter includes case studies full of examples and ideas, showcasing animal-based lesson planning, examples of common barriers and how they're overcome, and information about activities, projects and outcomes that have worked well.

It might feel like a long road since you started your planning, but once the animals arrive, the journey is only just beginning. Over the next few pages, you'll find real-world case studies - stories sharing both inspiration and tangible applications. Writing this section of the book has been our favourite, and it's full of lessons that have been planned, tested and loved, and details of real creative projects that sparked joy and learning, including honest reflections on the challenges that cropped up along the way.

So, grab a cuppa, a comfortable seat and your favourite pen for making notes - it's story time.

Riverside Education: A Whole-School Approach to Animal-Assisted Learning

Background

Riverside Education's first school building opened in 2015 with a desire to do something different. The original concept was centred around food and cookery, but when the building proved unsuitable, the team revisited their objectives and found another way to achieve them.

The original plan was designed to help foster a sense of cohesion at school, where everyone had a common set of experiences to use as a reference point and where this 'common ground' could shape and contextualise the learning.

The Challenge

Riverside's learners are a range of young people including those with SEN aged 14-19, and their mission is to 'develop potential in all young people' through providing a therapeutic, stimulating and practical learning environment that is interesting and fun.

Although there aren't many subject areas as universal as food, when the first group of learners arrived, they were asked about themselves, and the team noticed that most of the young people had pets or a love of animals, which soon reshaped the school's identity. A few reptiles and spiders in a classroom corner were enough to ignite joy and curiosity... and that spark changed everything.

Attendance improved, engagement deepened, and the young people began to see school as a place of connection and care. As the provision grew, the animals moved from a classroom into a dedicated farm space where students could study horticulture, animal care and equine studies, and the school's curriculum is now interwoven with daily animal routines, giving learners practical skills, emotional regulation and real pathways to future careers.

Approach

Empowering Learners

Riverside's philosophy is led by listening, both to the children and their support network and to the animals. The daily rhythms of the farm are predictable, purposeful and empowering. Students take ownership of their tasks and, with the use of a checklist or daily briefing, take charge of feeding, cleaning, monitoring and learning. During their time at the school, the learners have developed their understanding of what needs to be done and their sense of responsibility. The work helps to build confidence, teamwork and vocational capability in a way that traditional classrooms often struggle to achieve.

Importantly, the animal provision is not a side project. Although they came to school after it was opened, their presence runs through everything that happens here... and the curriculum has grown to match. Learners now study science through lambing, literacy through record-keeping, and maths through feed measurements. Administering medications teaches children about ratios, and for young people who have sometimes felt alienated by education, this real-world learning helps nebulous and abstract topics feel meaningful and alive.

But it didn't always look this way. When the animals were first introduced, the school's team took a 'wait and see' approach to designing learning. Remember when we talked about staying agile in your planning? That's the way that Riverside's headteacher, Abide Zenenga, approaches teaching and learning.

'When you open a school, you have an idea of how you want to do things, but the building will shape those plans. Then the children come, and they'll also shape and change the plans,' says Abide. So, just as plans changed when the school building wouldn't accommodate kitchen-based classrooms, once the animals arrived and were set up in their new homes, the team waited and observed as learners started to interact with the animals… And while watching, they listened.

'I wish we could get a rabbit.'

'I want to feed the snake.'

'At home, I like to…'

Integrating Learning with Practicality

These interactions helped to shape how learning developed around the animal provision. Weights, measures and ratios could support maths learning during feeding routines, discussions about why it's not a good idea to get only one rabbit helped to scaffold the learners' understanding of animal habitats, behaviours and emotions, and the young people expressed care and excitement in ways that were often absent from more traditional learning conversations.

Making Real Progress

What happened next was transformative. Children who had struggled to attend began turning up early, desperate to feed or check on their animals. The team recognised that the animals were changing behaviour and leaned in, setting up rotas so that the young people had a designated animal to care for and knew that if they didn't attend, their animal wouldn't receive the same level of care.

As the impact became clear, the school expanded the offer. Abide connected with others working in the field, and the team began to explore what a fuller animal provision might look like.

Eventually, the opportunity to acquire a farm came up. Despite knowing it would be a logistical and financial challenge, they went for it. The entire animal provision moved out of the classroom and on to a dedicated site, where pupils could engage in a far broader range of learning: horticulture, equine studies, animal care and farming.

Challenges

While the successes are clear, Abide is candid about the difficulties. Securing planning permission for a school on a farm took four years and was very expensive. Some community members were sceptical about a special school arriving in a rural area and the welfare of the animals.

But rather than becoming defensive, Riverside sought accountability. They now welcome six-monthly visits from the RSPCA, staff undertake continual training, and animal care decisions are collaborative, sometimes involving four trained staff with four different opinions. 'You have to learn to manage disagreement,' Abide says. 'And you have to do it ethically.' With a large number of different animals on site, vet bills are constant and high. Staff opinions sometimes clash. And every Christmas Day and New Year's morning, someone still has to tend the animals.

But Abide holds steady. 'You're going to have a lot of people challenge you,' he says. 'You just need to be sure you're doing the right thing… and do it anyway.'

A Whole-School Approach

The way that Abide embraces challenge is a hallmark of the 'whole-school' approach to planning. The collaboration between parents, learners and the local community is incredible, and everyone plays their part in the success of the school.

A different sort of challenge arose in the sheer amount of learning involved in developing an animal provision that was truly supportive of the animals, as well as the learners. The team have spent a lot of time planning animal housing and making sure that they properly understand the needs of the animals that they take on.

'You have to put yourself in the animals' shoes,' says Abide. 'A snake and a rat shouldn't be kept in the same room, for example,' he explains. 'The rat is living in fear – if the snake escapes, he'll be eaten – and the snake is being tortured with food that's constantly just out of reach.'

And this combination of 'figure it out as we go' and in-depth research is a true embodiment of agile planning. Riverside's animal provision didn't come from a strategic vision document, but from observation, responsiveness and courage. And in this way, it offers a powerful case study for any educator or leader considering animal-assisted practice or rethinking their setting.

Results and Impact

Riverside has become a haven for young people who had previously struggled with formal education. Learners now come in early, not because they have to, but because their animals are waiting. Pupils build confidence and vocational skills, and some have gone on to pursue careers in farming, veterinary care or land-based studies.

Even the animals themselves are thoughtfully chosen, with a growing interest in rare and specialist breeds. Through this additional lens, learners can gain a knowledge and understanding of genetics, breeding cycles, ethical care and climate challenges.

Rare and heritage breeds often display distinct physical characteristics - unusual colourings, fleece textures or body shapes that can spark curiosity and open the door to exploring genetics.

Learning Through Practice

Children can see for themselves how traits are inherited. For example, they might observe how the curly fleece of a Valais Blacknose sheep is passed down through a breeding line, or learn how dominant and recessive traits affect things like beak colour in chickens or coat markings in goats.

By linking what they see in the animals to basic genetic principles, children who may struggle with abstract concepts in a textbook can begin to understand how inheritance works. They might even begin to explore how genetic diversity supports species health and learn that some rare breeds are preserved precisely because of their resilient gene pools.

Working with rare or heritage animals gives children the opportunity to learn about reproduction, birth and life cycles in a safe, supported and ethical way. Unlike more generic animal care courses that may cover mating and reproduction in theory, working with rare breeds often involves planning for breeding season, monitoring animal health and supporting the young through critical early stages.

Learners grow to recognise the signs of pregnancy, understand gestation periods and talk about breeding as part of conservation. For learners with additional social development needs, caring for pregnant or young animals can build a deep sense of empathy, responsibility and connection.

Lessons Learned

Riverside is proof that transformative education doesn't need a polished five year plan. It needs people willing to listen, to adapt and to follow the path that emerges. With patience, trust and a strong sense of ethics, visions can often bring themselves to life.

Start where you are. It might be a class pet, a patch of outdoor space or a few enthusiastic colleagues. Build from there and stay open to where your learners might lead you.

The Riverside model proves that when education is shaped around the needs of learners, extraordinary things can happen. By starting with the passions and interests of students, and building trust over time, the school has developed a model that's both academically rigorous and deeply human. Emotional literacy, life skills and vocational preparation are embedded in the everyday rhythms of the farm.

> Where are you starting from? List what you have, however small, and think about how you could use it to get started. What else do you need before you get started and what can wait until your learners show you the way?

Emzi Mills-Frater: Building an Animal Education Centre

Emzi Mills-Frater is a passionate leader with a career spanning more than 15 years across further and higher education, STEM engagement and the charity sector. From managing adoption centres to developing national qualification standards, Emzi has consistently championed ethical, learner-centred and practically driven animal education, describing herself as interested in everything 'from digital space to nature-based education and all in between'.

After working in a number of roles which involved outreach and a focus on science and STEM, she started a role with Petroc College in North Devon to lead the creation of a new animal management department with just a small team, transforming a blank slate into a functioning education and welfare space within just a few months.

Background

Emzi's background in zoology definitely gave her a head start when implementing an animal-based project, but there were still numerous challenges to overcome in the planning and implementation of the college's first ever animal project, including around the mundane and ordinary aspects of change, like gaining access to the setting out of hours and during holidays so that the animals could be fed and cared for.

Emzi brought experience of working in higher education for a role where her focus was widening access and participation particularly in areas of low representation and engagement, and an understanding of animal behaviour, but many of the obstacles were new, by virtue of this project being a trailblazer… just like the one you might be considering building in your own setting.

The Challenge

Emzi and her team were tasked with establishing a new animal education centre to deliver qualifications that were specifically around animal provision. With a deadline from July to September, the project involved designing and building an animal facility from scratch (housing, tanks, aviaries) in a prefab building, sourcing suitable animals ethically, launching Level 2 and 3 animal care and management courses, and getting ready to support an initial cohort of 20 students, many of whom had struggled to learn in traditional classroom settings.

Although it might have seemed insurmountable to be presented with all of these challenges at once, Emzi took an iterative approach to balancing the complex demands of animal welfare, student progression and institutional expectations, and was able to take each hurdle in turn, to make sure that the setting was delivered successfully… and, oh boy, was it successful!

Approach

Ethics and Animal Welfare

The team started by building partnerships with zoos, farms and charities to rehome animals ethically. This minimised the commercial purchase of animals and embedded animal welfare and social value throughout the curriculum. It gave Emzi the opportunity to talk with learners where the animals came from, discuss the ethics of animal trade and connect these discussions in the classroom to the practical side of learning. However, there are additional challenges that come with working in this way. Donated and rehomed animals are sometimes less socialised or may even have experienced abuse or neglect in previous homes. This means that they require careful behaviour management, planning for enrichment and flexibility in lesson delivery to make sure that they're able to spend time with learners safely and without distress.

Another challenge here is that it's important to know which animals you're going to house before you build an environment for them, so you can have that suitable environment ready when they arrive. This applies not just to polar opposite species housing – for example, a goat and a bearded dragon – but those with more similar requirements such as a hamster and a gerbil. A similar set-up might work to minimum requirements, but to teach and promote the right values, you want to optimise their enclosure, in this case for potential group living and the ability to burrow for the gerbil. Developing a relationship with local organisations meant that Emzi could work with them to rehome the animals from selecting the right species to getting to know the individual animal's temperament and needs, and know that they were safe and well cared for, while she got the classroom environment ready for them to arrive in their new home.

When risk assessing your project, considering whether bought animals that can be socialised in your environment from a young age or rescued animals which allow for more diverse interactions are the best option for the animals, your learners and your own abilities and needs. If you do need to buy animals, you could consider how to use your decision-making process as a discussion point or learning topic for your learners.

Inclusive, Practical Education

Emzi had anticipated that students enrolled on an animal management course would enjoy practical sessions with animals, but was surprised to find that even during theory lessons, simply being in the animal room had a noticeably calming effect. Students appeared more regulated, less anxious and, in some cases, were even less distracted than in a standard classroom, despite not directly interacting with the animals. These positive effects were especially noticeable during high-pressure periods, such as assignment deadlines, The team then found themselves challenging conventional scheduling for classroom timetables and pushed back against restrictions that worked for other subjects; animal care, as we see in other contexts, sometimes just needs customised provision. Maybe it was the less formal setting or the presence of the animals, but it became obvious that the lessons which took place within the animal classroom had better outcomes for teaching. The space was less restrictive for learners who struggled with traditional classroom environments. It offered more purposeful context, with the students seeing in the animal set-up how the theory they were learning directly linked into practice. Students engaged more readily with tasks and even noise levels improved (somewhat!) with the class recognising that many animals, especially reptiles, are sensitive to sound or vibrations.

After the initial risk assessment and set-up was completed and learners became more confident, students co-produced risk assessments, learned to handle feed and bedding loads, and learned about PPE and infection control as part of their day-to-day, all while learning the theory behind the practice to support their qualification. Making links with other departments meant that Emzi was able to bring health and safety learning to life by providing UV handwashing demos with the childcare department, showing learners the impact of handwashing, rather than just the theory behind why it matters. This helped to embed health and safety thinking into daily routines, reinforcing both the focus on qualifications and life skills.

Strategic Relationships

Other great examples of building strategic relationships to support the project included a working agreement with the public services and outdoor studies departments to share the exercise space for animal training and dog agility, rather than seeking separately allocated provision. Demonstrating this flexibility and ability to collaborate across the college made it easier to secure access to resources and allowed the team to offer more when working with other partners. In this case, gaining access to the field allowed animals to exercise and students to spend time with the dogs and goats outdoors, in a safe fenced environment, without needing to arrange sessions off-site.

Local businesses were also keen to get involved with the project, once up and running, and made donations of equipment and resources, so that they could be associated with the work and give back to their local community, and the same charities who had been involved in animal rehoming and fostering pitched in by delivering talks and training to learners, staff and the local community at the animal centre

Strong, Values-Driven Team Culture

As the success of the provision grew, so did the offer, and from starting with a small number of animals in a prefab, the team developed an offer which included animal management, land-based studies, dog grooming and other qualifications, and brought together the college and its neighbours through offering services to the local community. While locals benefited from reduced-price dog grooming, the learners were never short of volunteer models for their practice and assessment needs.

But there were challenges here too. The college's overarching health and safety policy meant that dogs were excluded from the premises, but it's pretty impossible to deliver a dog-grooming qualification without access to dogs to groom!

Approaching this as a logistical challenge rather than getting frustrated at what seemed like a problem with a simple solution when a resolution was not quickly forthcoming, Emzi and her team dove into policy development and business casing, showing the need for and potential benefits of allowing dogs on to the premises. Within their case, they explained the benefits to learner wellbeing, the need for regular observation and assessment with dogs on site, and the potential financial benefits of expanding the animal provision to include the dog-grooming qualification.

At the same time as selling the requirement for the rules to be changed, the team needed to address the risks that the rule was made to mitigate. Developing signage, ensuring dogs were kept on leads when not in designated areas and educating dog owners on care and etiquette not only helped to mitigate these risks, but also provided valuable learning opportunities. The customer-facing interactions students could then have enabled them to meet the practical requirements of their course and gain the hands-on experience needed to become confident in their work placements and roles in the industry.

As the small team settled in that first year, Emzi, Lucy and Holli worked closely together, each bringing different strengths from backgrounds in equine and veterinary care, non-profits and higher education. Though at similar stages in their careers, it was this diversity and a shared commitment to animal welfare that created the trust and determination needed to move the project forward. Fittingly, the first three rabbits rehomed on site were named after them, reflecting the personal investment and care each team member brought right from the beginning.

Together, the small team navigated the teething issues and organisational ambiguity with openness and resolve. They created a working culture where it was safe to challenge decisions and stay curious in the face of complexity, to prioritise both animal and student welfare. Even difficult paperwork or policies became opportunities to ask the right questions and shape better practice.

There was never a question of whether the project would succeed, only how. By understanding what sat behind a 'no', the team often uncovered what was needed to turn it into a 'yes'. That mindset, paired with unwavering mutual support for each other, ensured that animals received the highest standards of care, learners were well supported, and aspirations could be raised.

Results and Impact

As a result of being able to employ an agile approach to the project, a fully operational animal unit with secure housing, enrichment spaces and tailored student access protocols was launched over the course of the summer holidays, on time and on budget.

Students who previously struggled in academic settings flourished in the practical sessions, and animals supported learners to communicate, learn and self-regulate. The team saw increased confidence ownership of own learning and enthusiasm from learners who might previously have struggled to engage in classroom settings. In time, they were even able to collaborate with the high-profile organisation Blue Cross to open a cat adoption programme of their own from site!

Starting small, the original project was able to grow and expand beyond the two groups on Level 2 Animal Care and Level 3 Animal Management. After the initial project was shown to be successful, plans were approved for dog-grooming qualifications and wider community outreach, animal rehoming and collaborative ventures with other departments and organisations.

 Think! How could you start small and grow your animal provision? Would a tank of stick insects be easier to sell to your leadership team than a classroom dog? Try to consider ways that you can demonstrate the value of animal provision incrementally, just like Emzi did.

One step at a time, Emzi and her team helped shift college-wide assumptions around timetabling, classroom structures and learner capability, building the case for investment through demonstrated value. Where might your first animal lead?

Lessons Learned

Ethics must be non-negotiable, particularly when animals are involved. Students absorb values as well as knowledge, and demonstrating your values in your work, through the way that animals' five welfare needs are met and in the way you talk about any conflicts between animal welfare, learner needs and current policy will help you to demonstrate the consistency of your values and build trust. Animal-based practice only works when the needs of the animal come first. This focus on seeking to understand the needs of the animal and always showing up in their corner is a key way that animal interactions help to build trust between practitioners and learners, instil knowledge and values, and open the door to conversations where learners can share their own needs and experiences.

The right environment can change everything. When animal welfare is consistently prioritised, learners see that care in action. They understand that they are expected to show the same level of responsibility and respect for the animals, and they also come to recognise that their own wellbeing is prioritised by the team too. By experiencing the thoughtful planning and attention to safety for the animals, learners come to feel a sense of physical and emotional safety themselves. When learners feel safe and cared for, it becomes possible to unlock their potential.

Cross-organisational partnerships drive innovation, whether internal or in the wider community. From handwashing demos to co-designed spaces, a lot of the success of the animal management project came down to the continued will to collaborate and solve problems together with others. Emzi was able to build a true community around the animal provision within the college, making the experience of studying and living in the area a richer one. Where might local partnerships aid your success? Are there businesses or settings that you could start to build a relationship with to help you get your ideas up and running?

Blue-sky thinking works best when grounded in reality, and while the college was genuinely invested in supporting the animal provision, a big change inevitably needs adjustments to how things are done. There were challenges in policy implementation, logistics and in the nitty-gritty, day-to-day realities of making the 'big vision' possible. When developing provision that includes any living thing, creativity is essential, but the project must be scoped for sustainability – remember, a shared vision and willingness to challenge each other constructively makes ambitious work possible.

Emzi and her team's work is an excellent blueprint for values-led animal education projects, where welfare, student needs and real-world practice are all important parts of the puzzle. By rethinking what education can look like and using challenges as springboards for new ideas, she proves here that ethical, inclusive and practical learning is not only possible, but can prove transformative for settings and learners alike.

Lesley Forrester: Northern Animal Assisted Therapies and Activities (NAATA)

Lesley Forrester is an animal-assisted speech and language therapist based in the North-East of England. Her deep compassion for both children and animals has allowed her to forge her own, fairly unique, career journey from being a speech and language therapist in a traditional therapy setting into a career in animal-assisted education, offering animal experiences and interventions to schools to help to develop skills of all kinds in children who might need extra support. Working with schools, SEND settings and nurseries, Lesley has developed a practice which allows children to interact with therapy dogs and chickens, and supports children to thrive socially, emotionally and communicatively. Her Community Interest Company (CIC), Northern Animal Assisted Therapies and Activities (NAATA), primarily works with school settings and nurseries, and leads projects which are determined by the needs of the children and animals taking part. Her approach blends responsive, flexible planning with clear ethical standards and clearly documented safeguarding practices, and through her work with a team of therapy dogs, Lesley helps to create spaces where children feel seen, trusted and empowered to be themselves.

Background

Lesley began her career as a speech and language therapist. Long hours working within the NHS meant that she couldn't ethically have a dog of her own, but once established in her career and confident in her ability to work with children, she found a way to bring her two loves together to create something unique. Recognising the rising mental health and communication needs in children, Lesley shifted toward animal-assisted therapy and founded her own practice.

Despite being a confident and competent therapist, her transition wasn't without challenges, and balancing the demands of self-employment, client expectations and animal welfare meant she had to advocate strongly for ethical practices and resist shortcuts. It would have been easy to try to squeeze a lot into the day, but being conscious of the needs of the dogs and hens means limiting their activity and caring for their needs before considering business demands.

Lesley believes that a solid foundation in either therapy or education is vital before layering in animals, ensuring both the child and the animal are supported. There's a lot to learn about working with children and animals, and it might be too much to try to embed all of that learning at once, with two totally different groups to care for.

Think! Do you feel confident enough in your ability to understand and connect with your learners before introducing animals? How would you recognise the signs that they weren't comfortable or needed help? Would you know when to intervene in their play or how to scaffold their learning in an organic environment? Before you introduce animals into your setting, it's important that you know yourself and your learners well enough to be able to predict and respond to their needs and behaviours with relative confidence.

The Challenge

Animal-assisted activities are becoming increasingly popular in schools and educational settings, and Lesley identified that sometimes there can be a lack of clarity and preparation in how these initiatives are rolled out. There needs to be clear guidance to protect both children and animals. In particular, Lesley raised concerns about dogs being introduced into classrooms without adequate planning, support or understanding of their limits, highlighting that compromised animal welfare could ultimately endanger children too.

Lesley works with schools that aren't able to have their own animal provision, or settings that might be looking for specialist interventions for children who need support hitting specific educational milestones or learning outcomes. NAATA have provided support with a wide range of objectives from structured support for functional maths, for those students struggling with numeracy, through to therapeutic interventions within nurture groups, focused upon fostering friendships and building confidence and communication skills.

> Are you able to confidently provide support to your learners and a classroom animal? Can you fulfil the needs of a classroom animal as a priority, or do your learners need your primary attention? Would engaging an external animal provision be more beneficial at the beginning of your animal journey, to help you grow your confidence and build a case for the benefits of introducing animals full-time?

Approach

For Lesley, the ethics of allowing animals and children to interact are non-negotiable. Keeping everyone safe relies on being able to put the animal's needs first. Her sessions are built around understanding and respecting the dogs' instincts and signals. She draws a sharp distinction between therapy animals and classroom pets, warning against keeping dogs in school for extended periods without breaks or proper welfare considerations, which might be the case where teachers are required to stay with groups of learners and there's a risk that animal needs will come secondary to the comfort and safety of the learners.

Lesley lets her dogs lead the activities and the pace of engagement. Her own dogs are not forced into rigid roles; rather, they are supported to be themselves, which is an approach she has found to be more powerful than traditional 'obedience-based' training.

The two dogs that work with Lesley are different from one another. There's an older dog, who is calm and highly trained. She can do various engaging tricks and tasks, and she's happy to disengage and show that she's 'done' at the end of her time interacting with children. Lesley's younger dog was socialised in a different way and trained more around relationships. He is less rigidly trained and more able to respond to the needs and moods of the children, but less able to self-regulate and recognise his own needs, meaning that Lesley has to be aware of his energy levels and comfort, because he's likely to push himself too far. Being able to understand and interact with your animals in this way is crucial to a successful animal project, especially in the long term, and you're going to need to spend time getting to know how your animals signal their feelings of discomfort or displeasure, both to keep them safe and well, and to successfully negate any safety concerns which might arise from overworked or overtired animals being asked to do more.

Responsive, Child-Led Practice

Lesley's model is based on flexible planning. She often brings a trolley of resources to a session with a loose idea of what might unfold, but she follows the lead of the children and the dogs to adapt the session to their needs and mood. In one example, children in a SEND setting were braiding fabric together to build dexterity and proprioception, with a more able learner paired with someone who needed more support; while learners were discussing their improvements and showing off their finished plaits, one of the dogs was keen to join in, taking the braided material and running outside ready to instigate a game of 'tug of war'.

Instead of trying to get this activity back on track, Lesley went with it, asking the children to consider how excited the dog might be with the new toy that they had made for him, and what he might be feeling at that moment.

Her sessions are careful to allow space for authentic connection like this, moments where children and animals can simply 'be', building trust and emotional regulation by spending time in the presence of a calm, responsive dog. Lesley believes in allowing children to define their own outcomes and shares that real skill lies in knowing when to guide and when to let things be.

Although this comes fairly easily to Lesley now, it's important to recognise the skills that she brought with her from her NHS therapy practice, reading behaviour, anticipating need and recognising distress in those who might not be able to comfortably or confidently communicate it. Again, it's important to consider where you are in your own confidence journey. Animal-based education might seem like a good way to bridge the gap between you and your learners, but it's important that you already understand their needs and behaviours before introducing animals to the setting.

As well as bringing a lot of experience in reading behaviour and building communication skills with children, Lesley does a lot of preparation for sessions, and a lot of following up. Communication with teachers, parents and the participants helps to shape sessions and to keep everyone safe. Lesley knows that she's working with a good school when they're communicative and willing to involve parents in the development of sessions. Questionnaires are sent home to gather information about children's needs, fears, allergies and behaviours, and teachers contribute knowledge of children's educational goals and challenges, to help Lesley to design sessions in a way that will support everyone.

Could you consider working with an external provider while building your own project plan? Taking time to understand what successful animal providers consider, plan for and require might help you to better implement a project that supports your learners and caters well for the needs of the animals taking part. Consider contacting local providers to talk about how they work and find out whether your school might be a suitable place to engage them in an initial project to assess how your learners, colleagues and parents respond.

Strategic Practice and Safeguarding

Lesley stresses the importance of robust safeguarding frameworks. She works closely with schools to ensure that clear documentation, parental consent and policies are in place. By targeting schools with an existing therapeutic ethos, Lesley ensures alignment with her values and reduces friction in embedding her work. Considering the environment of your school, how well would Lesley's approach work for your learners? Would you need to adapt your setting's approach to policy or planning?

The presence of dogs is not just emotionally supportive – it's educationally beneficial. We've talked about some of the ways that animals can scaffold learning, and depending on the aims of the project, Lesley might incorporate practical tasks like creating tally charts of animal behaviours or food or distance measurement into sessions involving dogs. Embedding learning into play and animal interaction provides neurodivergent and anxious children with meaningful, grounded learning opportunities which help develop maths skills or science knowledge without being too intimidating.

Lesley recommends starting small with pilot projects or one-off sessions to allow both school and practitioner to test the waters before committing to long-term delivery. Preparation, she says, takes three times longer than the actual sessions, but it's vital to ensuring success, especially when the plan needs to remain flexible. You have to be able to anticipate and respond to any eventuality without losing control.

Results and Impact

Lesley's approach has seen incredible outcomes. Children who were previously withdrawn or struggling with communication begin to express themselves around animals, often through reading animal body language or interpreting subtle behaviours. Dogs can become catalysts for empathy, language development and self-regulation, or lead to children feeling comfortable enough to talk for the first time.

Her model also empowers dogs. Both dogs are enabled to act upon their own drives and be their authentic self, but Lesley has focused much more upon this and less upon training behaviours in Gunther's preparation for work. Behaviours such as leave, down stays and taking treats gently are crucial for safety and, clearly some trained behaviours are a must and non-negotiable in school settings. But over-training dogs can interfere with them expressing their own personalities and play preferences, and the result of Lesley's approach is a richer, more natural interaction that benefits both the dogs (who can act as a team) and the learners (who get to interact with two very different and distinct personalities).

Lesley's work is reshaping perceptions of animal-assisted interventions, advocating for a shift from novelty to necessity, and she hopes to see that animal-assisted interactions are introduced in education settings where practitioners are equipped with the insight, reflection and ethics required to keep the needs of the animal at the forefront of their delivery.

Think! Are your animal-assisted sessions truly mutual? Are you creating space for both the child and the animal to lead, adapt and feel safe? Could starting with a short pilot project help you refine your practice and demonstrate value to your setting?

Lessons Learned

It's important to prioritise ethics over excitement. Animal-assisted education is only effective when animals are not seen as tools, but as equal participants in sessions. Welfare needs must come first, and it's important that the animals enjoy their time with the children to make the session beneficial for everyone. Ask yourself: What is the dog getting out of this task or activity?

Authenticity builds trust, and both children and animals thrive when they can be themselves. Over-training can diminish spontaneity and richness in the interactions, but under-training can mean that dogs aren't equipped for the interactions that they have with children. Finding a balance where everyone feels as though they're able to shape the session and interact safely can help build relationships and skills much more quickly.

Preparation is everything and, behind every 30-minute session lie hours of thoughtful planning, safeguarding and emotional preparation. The more flexible the delivery, the more structured the foundations must be to make sure that things don't get out of hand. While it's important for children and animals to lead the activity and feel comfortable expressing their needs, Lesley's role is to scaffold, shape and anticipate what might come next, and this can only happen if she knows the needs of the group, the capabilities of the animals and the structure of her activities inside out.

Not all schools are ready to work in an animal-centred way. Lesley seeks out settings with a therapeutic mindset and will push back against environments that see dogs as cute novelties rather than sensitive co-facilitators. Is your setting ready to fully embrace animal-supported delivery, including working with the animals and accommodating their needs as a priority, or do you still have work to do in changing hearts and minds about the way that animal-assisted activities could support your learners' development?

Lesley's journey shows that values-led, small-scale beginnings can evolve into sustainable, high-impact practices, as long as they're rooted in reflection and mutual respect. By combining clinical or educational skill with a deep understanding of animal behaviour and a fierce commitment to child agency, it is possible to change what education can look like, as long as you're willing to cede some control to your animals.

Jayne Haigh: Goxhill Meadows Hearts and Minds

Jayne Haigh didn't set out to build a business. In fact, when she first left teaching, she had no concrete plans at all, just a deep love for animals, a smallholding in rural Yorkshire, and a desire to help children who, like some she'd taught, needed something different. That seed of intention, planted gently in the uncertainty of change, has grown into Goxhill Meadows Hearts and Minds: a thriving, trauma-informed, animal-assisted education and therapeutic activity setting that supports some of the most vulnerable young people in her region.

From Minty the lamb, who helped a withdrawn Year 6 pupil open up during a school leavers' assembly, to Flynn the horse, Jayne's work has been grounded in care, curiosity and commitment. Today, her team supports children with complex emotional needs, many of whom are non-speaking, are neurodivergent, or have experienced significant trauma. Jayne has a thriving business with lots of incoming requests, but she doesn't do any advertising at all... and never has done!

Background

Jayne's journey began while she was still a teacher. During her final year working as a teacher in a primary school, a rescued lamb named Minty made an unexpected impact. Taken into school as a stop-gap solution during the Easter holidays, after being bottle-reared on Jayne's smallholding, Minty visited every classroom and was cared for by students and colleagues. At the end-of-year leavers' assembly, one of the school's challenging pupils stood up and happily declared: 'The best thing about my time at school was Minty the lamb.' That single sentence really made an impact on Jayne, and it's stayed with her ever since.

Shortly after she started to seriously consider the potential impact of animals on children's wellbeing and learning, Jayne left teaching and began offering glamping facilities and interactive animal experiences on her smallholding. During lockdown, families came to the farm, drawn not just by the scenery but by the ability to interact with the animals who live there and share wholesome and supportive experiences with their children. When Jayne invited children to the farm to meet the animals, parents began to notice changes in their self-confidence, their willingness to engage and interact, and their behaviour, particularly for those who found communication or formal settings difficult to navigate. And Jayne's care and attention soon meant that what started as a leisure business, offering informal meet-the-animals experiences for families, became something deeper when one family asked whether Jayne could support their child, who had been diagnosed as autistic, more regularly. The setting at Goxhill Meadows is one that's based in nurture. All of the children are treated with unconditional positive regard – there is no judgement. They are seen, valued and belong, from the first time that they visit.

The Challenge

Jayne's business is now a commissioned provider of animal-assisted support, because when she started out, her background in education and obvious care for her animals was what led to increasing referrals and growing demand from families, schools and local authorities. Because of the demand, she had to find a way to professionalise, formalise and scale her business to meet it, without losing the heart and soul of what made Goxhill Meadows special.

Jayne needed to find ways to support children with significant trauma or additional needs in a safe, ethical and effective way. Jayne's ethics meant that it was important to her that she advocate for animal welfare as equal to (and sometimes a model for) human wellbeing. And managing rapid growth while staying rooted in the original values of her offer was a challenge that needed support from others, leading to the eventual recruitment of colleagues with complementary skills to those that Jayne started out with.

Approach

Start with the Animals, Always

For Jayne and her team, animal welfare is not negotiable. Every session begins with checking in not just with the young person but with the animal. Are they calm? Do they want to engage? Are they well? If the answer is no, they rest. There aren't only opportunities for learning when engaging directly with the animal. When the animals aren't feeling up to it, new opportunities are presented. Instead of interacting with the animals when the animals aren't interested, Jayne encourages children to observe them in their natural rest and play. Watching the animals with the children allows Jayne to ask, 'What do you think they're feeling?' and 'How might they react if...?' As well as learning about social cues and practising the reading of non-verbal communication in others, many children are able to recognise their own emotions in the animals, sometimes before they can name them in themselves.

Trauma-Informed and Child-Led

After completing a Level 6 Diploma in Equine Facilitated Psychotraumatology (EFPT), Jayne designed Goxhill's approach to be truly trauma-informed. That means the team doesn't offer trauma therapy, but they do provide the essential first steps of safety, stability and relationship building. Many children arrive at Goxhill stuck in a fight-or-flight loop; being trauma-informed helps to make sure that while they're on site, they learn how to co-regulate through both animal interaction and conversation with adults that they learn to trust.

One of Jayne's foundational strategies is teaching through metaphor and mirroring. 'If that horse is pacing in the stable, what might he be feeling?' she asks. 'Can you think of a time that you have felt like that?' Slowly and gently, this helps children who might struggle to identify their feelings to start to make links to their bodies, their emotions and their behaviours.

Relationships First, Paperwork Second (But Not Forgotten)

The structure of Goxhill Meadows is held together by a small and highly skilled team. One staff member is a former SENCO, another a veterinary nurse and former teaching assistant; together, they bring professional rigour to the warmth of the space. The team works closely with schools, NHS services and local authorities to ensure that safeguarding, data sharing and evaluation are watertight.

> What does your professional network look like? Who could you rely on to help you navigate the logistics of animal provision in your setting? Actively building a network that supports your personal learning and provides opportunities for collaboration can help keep your project sustainable and fun.

Although 95 per cent of young people are now funded through education, health and care plans (EHCPs) or healthcare commissioning, Jayne still sees the work that Goxhill do as being primarily relationship-driven. 'It's not about the forms,' she says. 'It's about the child, the animal, and the trust between them.'

> Have you looked into what funding might be available for your project through your local authority, healthcare services or community funds? While it's important to keep the focus on the children and animals, understanding how your project will remain financial sustainable can help to take the pressure off.

Because Goxhill Meadows is registered as a private business, Jayne is licensed under statutory guidance, which means that an inspector from the local authority has visited the site to complete an inspection, in accordance with regulation 10 requirements of the Animal Welfare (Licensing of Activities Involving Animals) (England) Regulations 2018.

Jayne believes that anyone who is able to should pursue licensing, even when they aren't obliged to, as it provides an additional layer of guidance and governance to help settings remain focused on the needs of the animals and encourages everyone to stay up to date with best practice to help with continuous improvement.

Jayne is also a member of Horses in Therapy and Education International (HETI) who hold rigorous standards for any individual or organisation offering equine-assisted interventions, which means that she is registered on the UK Human and Equine Interaction Register (HEIR).

Is licensing your animal activities something that you could pursue? Seek out the statutory guidance and any advice that's available from your local authority. If licensing isn't an option, or you're not ready to pursue this officially, could you use the guidance as a self-imposed standard to help keep your provision needs-focused?

Results and Impact

Goxhill Meadows now supports a wide range of children and young people, from those disengaged from mainstream education to children who are supported through foster care or residential childcare settings. Over time, many have transitioned from needing 4:2, 3:1 or 2:1 support ratios to 1:1, and several have successfully returned to mainstream school settings, which is a huge achievement for those previously considered too complex to place.

The animals are a big part of this story, with children able to build deep bonds with animals who help them to feel safe. Haku, a 25-year-old rescue horse with complex needs, built a remarkable bond with a young boy named Eddie. Their connection was so transformative that photos of them together still feature on Goxhill's website.

Because of these close relationships, it's critical that endings are done with care. When a child stops attending, whether due to a placement change, a funding shift or a transition, it's possible that the experience could be traumatic. A sudden end to children's ability to spend time with animals that they've grown to love has the potential to surface old feelings or to impact on the children's progress. To help to mitigate this, the team communicate well with children's guardians and other provision to make sure that they're well prepared to leave and to say goodbye when it's time – and they are sent away with a memory book full of photos, quotes and shared moments as a tangible reminder that their time at Goxhill mattered, and to help them to process the transition.

How can you make sure that children are ready to move on from your animal provision? What tools can you use or develop to help make the end of your animal project a positive one? How can colleagues and collaborators help with the transition away from animal provision to make children feel safe and cared for?

Lessons Learned

Co-regulation has to be the starting point. Children can't learn, reflect or connect if they don't feel safe. Every session at Goxhill Meadows starts with grounding, whether that's through listening to birdsong or standing quietly at the gate, making gentle observations about how the animals might feel. Nobody is allowed to approach the animals without first taking time to check in with themselves and their animal friends' behaviour.

The animals are teachers too. Flighty horses, cautious dogs and sleepy goats all have lessons to share, and Jayne uses their behaviour to teach children about emotional literacy, boundaries and empathy. Where might animals scaffold your lessons and add opportunities to slow down, observe and reflect?

Professionalism enables magic, and behind the wholesome and charming experience at Goxhill is a serious infrastructure. Safeguarding, consent, supervision and licensing are all part of the package and are critical for sustainability. Having a team with skills that complement each other is important. If everyone is focused on making an impact directly, it may become difficult to stay aware of business needs and licensing requirements or to properly explore potential opportunities as they arise.

Endings matter, and producing memory books, planning careful transitions and providing closure rituals can all help children process change and show that the relationship that have built with the animals wasn't transactional and they weren't 'just another client'.

Loss and grief are a natural part of life, but the experience of losing someone we love, whether human or animal, can be particularly impactful. When animals pass away, Goxhill supports children through the grieving process, using it as an opportunity to talk about compassion, kindness and saying goodbye. Reaching out to parents, guardians and educators, Goxhill ensures that children are supported before and after leaving sessions that involve emotional outcomes or discussions. How can you make sure that children's experiences in your setting are supported by their support network at home?

Jayne's journey from teacher to providing an in-demand service as an animal-assisted practitioner shows what can happen when care, courage and ethics come together. She proves that you don't need to start with a fully formed five-year plan to change lives, just a willingness to start with what you have and stay true to your values.

> Take some time to reflect on where you're starting. Write down what impact you're hoping to achieve with your initial animal provision and the hurdles that might get in your way. You'll soon have a list of initial goals, setting you on the right path to overcoming your obstacles and making your ideas a reality.

Jenny Phillips: Starting from Scratch

Jenny's work in animal-assisted provision began with a simple instinct: that children thrive in the company of animals. From stray cats to alpacas, micro pigs to snakes, Jenny has built rich, responsive learning experiences for children, particularly those with SEND, that centre around therapeutic and educational interactions with animals.

Background

Jenny's early experiments began in higher education, where she worked as a nurse educator. She introduced animals into her university lectures to help health professionals understand the importance of comfort, connection and emotional wellbeing, and took over lecture theatres and corridors with what she laughingly describes as a 'zoo', but her intent was grounded in evidence and impact. That success laid the foundations for more child-centred work, allowing her to test and develop models of animal-based learning and therapy within a forest school context.

Today, Jenny runs provision for young children that includes chickens, alpacas, snakes, cats and a dog, all carefully introduced and supported, bringing a trauma-informed, animal-assisted model into a classroom environment.

Figure 6.1 Friendly, fluffy chickens can make great animal companions

Approach

Know Your Animals

Jenny's approach to animal-assisted education is deeply ethical and highly practical. 'Know your animals. Know your people,' she says. Before any child is allowed to touch or work with an animal, Jenny has already spent time understanding both the animal's triggers and preferences and the child's developmental stage and sensory profile.

In one example, Jenny describes George, a temperamental rehomed cat who formed a unique and transformational bond with a child with Down syndrome. By introducing interactions slowly and purposefully, and supporting the child's motor skills, social understanding and emotional regulation, George became a co-teacher. He helped the child learn to make marks, use gentle hands and even understand conversation turn-taking. What looked like a friendship was also a curriculum in action.

Observing George taught Jenny that George didn't like being approached from the front, and preferred to be interacted with from one side. Showing, teaching and scaffolding how learners interacted with George allowed Jenny to demonstrate this care and empathy, model how to observe and assess animal behaviour, and teach learners how to replicate this for themselves, helping everyone to feel safe, supported and cared for.

Child-Led Interaction

For children who are fearful of animals, especially dogs, Jenny begins from a distance. Children are invited to observe the animal safely, noticing features like colour, size and movement, without being asked to engage. Over time, she brings them a little closer, to the tail end of a friendly dog, where children can see the tail wag and safely stroke without feeling overwhelmed. The goal is to make the interaction feel safe, predictable and child-led.

In the forest school setting, Jenny supports children to develop independence and responsibility through daily care routines, which include feeding the alpacas using flat hands to avoid nips, grooming sessions to encourage fine motor control and sensory regulation, and walking alpacas with double-handled leads, giving children real autonomy while staying safe.

Through these scaffolded and nested interactions, children learn to read animal body language as a foundation for interaction. They notice wagging tails, relaxed posture or signs that a cat or alpaca wants space. These activities not only support confidence-building around animals but also build emotional literacy and social understanding.

Sensory Learning

Jenny also uses different animals to support different sensory and emotional needs. Snakes and reptiles are slow-moving and quiet, which can make them ideal for children with auditory sensitivities or those needing calming pressure. Alpacas are warm, soft and steady, so they can offer deep-pressure input through touch and a safe sense of physical presence. Chickens and cats are responsive and relational, which can make them good for supporting empathy, gentle touch and nurturing behaviours. Chickens might seem like an odd pairing with cats, and you might be surprised to learn that happy chickens also purr. They can also be a little friendlier than cats, if they're handled while young, and are a good animal to encourage observation and relationship-based learning, while at the same time offering opportunities for handling, affection and bonding.

Children with sensory processing difficulties can benefit from these interactions by learning how different textures, sounds and rhythms affect their body and mind. Stroking a purring cat (or chicken!), for example, can help reset a child's homeostatic rhythm and offer a calming, grounding experience.

Never Assume

Jenny never assumes what will work. She encourages children to move among the animals freely and return to the ones they're drawn to, and observes how they move and interact. She also listens to personal histories: if a child had a pet rabbit growing up, she might introduce a guinea pig as a familiar but safe alternative. She also watches for subtle preferences. Which animal does the child look at most? Which one do they circle back to? Which one do they speak about afterwards? The goal isn't just to get children close to an animal, but to find the right match emotionally, cognitively and developmentally.

Jenny's experience extends beyond her own settings. She has participated in equine therapy sessions abroad and worked with micro pigs, which are highly intelligent, hypoallergenic animals that offer therapeutic benefits for children who may not be able to engage with more traditional pets. As part of her visit to an equine therapy centre in Bosnia, Jenny solidified her belief that animal interaction can be structured, ethical and transformative. Her exposure to the use of micro pigs in therapeutic work in the US, where pigs, rabbits, alpacas and even birds are used in hospitals, continues to inspire her vision for more diverse animal provision in UK health and education settings.

Lessons Learned

Start slowly and observe everything. Jenny teaches that the first step is always observation. Before introducing a child to an animal, she watches how they move, how they respond to noise or unpredictability, and how they express their emotions. 'Use your eyes, ears and brain cells first,' she says. Then she matches the child to the right animal, so that each is matched to one that moves at the right pace, has the right temperament and meets their needs.

Safety is non-negotiable, but fear is not a barrier. Many of Jenny's children have fears or phobias, but she never forces contact. Instead, she teaches children to name their fears, approach animals on their own terms and recognise that animals communicate through movement and posture. Those same lessons help children build resilience and trust in human relationships too.

You don't need a farm to start. Many of Jenny's most impactful interventions have taken place in modest forest school spaces or single classrooms. What matters most is not the size or number of animals, but the quality of the relationships and the intention behind the work.

Every animal has a role. Whether it's a purring cat, a huggable alpaca or a snake that soothes through pressure, Jenny uses the strengths of each species to meet different needs. Her learners are guided to discover the animal that meets them where they are, rather than being pushed into something unsuitable.

Ryan Perry: A First-Generation Farmer with a Passion for Rare Breeds and Public Service

Ryan Perry is a remarkable example of how passion, perseverance and ethical values can create a meaningful and sustainable animal-assisted pathway, even without access to large-scale resources or land.

As a first-generation farmer based in Gateshead, in the North-East of England, Ryan has built a thriving and thoughtful rare breeds enterprise alongside full-time shift work as a biomedical scientist.

His journey is not only a testament to the potential of small-scale conservation farming, but an inspiring model for career development that combines public service, agricultural heritage and a strong sense of community stewardship.

Background

Growing up on the edge of a 25-acre community farm, which was established on the banks of the River Tyne in the middle of a housing estate, Ryan was first introduced to livestock as a child, following the foot-and-mouth crisis in 2001. At just seven years old, he began volunteering and quickly formed deep bonds with the animals and people involved. The early days of feeding pigs and showing sheep sparked a lifelong interest in rare breeds and land stewardship, and over the years, this passion has never left him.

Ryan currently juggles a demanding science career with volunteer work and the care of his own livestock, including sheep, pigs, goats, cattle and poultry, across multiple locations in and around Gateshead.

Ryan's animal career began without access to any land or space of his own, but with a commitment to the animals he'd grown up with and a drive to keep rare breeds alive. His flock includes the descendants of sheep that he originally cared for as a child; today, those animals remain at the heart of his farming operation.

Figure 6.2 The Castlemilk Moorit is a small, primitive breed of lowland sheep which appears on the RBST watchlist

The Challenge

Farming Without a Farm

Farming without a farm presents its own unique challenges, many of which might apply in your setting. Ryan does not own a large permanent holding; instead, he works creatively across multiple sites, from local authority nature reserves to small fields borrowed through grazing agreements or offered in exchange for produce. This model of 'conservation grazing' not only supports his own herd's needs but also benefits biodiversity and land management efforts across the region.

It might be that your setting could adopt a similar model by approaching local authorities, environmental trusts, wildlife organisations or sympathetic landowners, and proposing educational partnerships.

Such partnerships could be framed around conservation education, linking the presence of animals to ecological stewardship. For example, native sheep breeds like the Hebridean and Whitefaced Woodland, used by Ryan, help manage rough pastureland by keeping invasive species in check, creating conditions where wildflowers and insects can flourish and replacing destructive grass trimmers and mowers so that migrating birds are able to nest and thrive. This kind of work has the potential to be deeply educational, and it links directly to science, geography and citizenship, providing real-world learning opportunities without requiring the school to own or maintain land themselves.

Space Costs Money – But So Does a Lack of It

A lack of space can pose a problem when it comes to finances too. Despite the possibility of saving money on grazing space, small enterprises like Ryan's also face higher costs for supplementary feed, such as hay and silage, as bulk purchases aren't possible due to lack of space and indoor storage. This can make costs unpredictable, with hay and silage costs being impacted by changes in the weather, transport costs and demand from larger farms. Ryan has to plan for all eventualities, to make sure that the animals always have everything that they need.

> How will your ability to buy hay or bedding be impacted by changes in the weather? If your animals live outside, and they need supplementary grass in winter, will you have somewhere to store bales of hay or straw for bedding? Consider what will happen in the most extreme of situations, as well as in the everyday.

Another key challenge for Ryan is time. Lambing season, pig farrowing and cattle-calving demands often overlap with his job, which involves shift work in a laboratory and providing training and development to apprentices, trainees and new colleagues. Ryan has found inventive ways to manage this, like organising his rota around lambing season, relying on trusted volunteers and neighbours for welfare checks, and employing more involved solutions, such as synchronising his breeding programmes using hormonal sponges to condense the sheep's birthing windows, meaning he can reliably take holiday from work for the two weeks that the sheep are due to deliver their lambs.

Whatever the challenge, however, Ryan is determined to make it work. He cares deeply about the animals he looks after and about their role in the wider ecosystem and food security, and he's keen to pass that learning on to others through working with schools, charities and through his volunteer work with the Rare Breed Survival Trust, where he is Vice-Chair of the Board of Trustees.

Figure 6.3 A Castlemilk Moorit sheep stays cosy inside with two fresh lambs

Approach

Start with Why

At the heart of Ryan's work is a deep love of rare and native breeds, not just for their aesthetic appeal but for their role in biodiversity, disease resistance and sustainable food production. He keeps Tamworth pigs, Shetland cattle and Bagot goats, all chosen for their heritage value and conservation status, among a number of other native and heritage breeds.

His dedication to breed preservation is meticulous and, where necessary, Ryan imports semen for artificial insemination to avoid keeping multiple boars, particularly in breeds with fewer lines. This might be another area that you want to consider in your own projects. If hatching programmes, lambing or other reproductive functionality is something you're keen to build into your learning programme, you'll need to consider what that might need to look like. Like boars, cockerels can be noisy and aggressive, but they can also provide protection and companionship for hens, and if you are breeding from any of your animals, you'll need to find a way to keep them separated, to make sure that there's no accidental in-breeding or unexpected babies.

This attention to detail and ethical consideration runs through every part of Ryan's practice.

Conservation and Education

Ryan's use of rare breeds is rooted in conservation, but he is also deeply committed to public understanding. As Vice-Chair of the Rare Breeds Survival Trust, he advocates nationally for their commercial viability and genetic importance, and locally, he educates neighbours, friends and the wider public about the role of native breeds in soil health, food security and sustainable farming.

In the context of food security, rare breeds offer genetic diversity. When food systems become overly reliant on a small number of genetically similar breeds, they also become more vulnerable to disease, climate shifts and changing environmental pressures. Rare and traditional breeds like the ones on Ryan's smallholding, tend to be hardier, more adaptable to local climates and better suited to low-input, sustainable farming systems. For example, while commercial pigs might thrive on concentrated feed in indoor conditions, rare breeds like the Tamworth or the Large Black are better foraged and more resilient in pasture-based settings, living outdoors all year round. This adaptability could become essential in the face of climate change or resource shortages.

Exploring Opportunities

From a practical teaching perspective, conserving rare breeds can provide rich learning opportunities. Children and young people can explore not only animal care but broader concepts like biodiversity, resilience and food sustainability. Activities might include exploring breed histories, mapping where animals originated and how they adapted to specific environments, or comparing different livestock for characteristics like feed conversion, temperament, or product quality (milk, wool, eggs, meat). These hands-on experiences ground abstract ideas in meaningful, sensory-rich learning.

History and Culture

Another area that Ryan highlights as important, which might not seem immediately obvious, is the link between animal breeds, history and culture.

Each rare breed carries with it a story of place, people and purpose. For example, the Suffolk Punch horse tells us about the days of heavy horse-powered agriculture in East Anglia. The Bagot goat traces its lineage to medieval deer parks and monastic estates. And the British Lop pig, with its calm temperament and large, floppy ears, speaks of small family farms and traditional pig-keeping in the South-West. These animals connect learners to their local landscapes and the communities that shaped them. For children, especially those who learn best through doing, caring for such animals is a way of stepping into a story and learning through relationship.

Curriculum Links

In practice, rare breeds can help children explore a range of curriculum-linked themes. A lesson centred on the Lincoln Longwool sheep, for example, could include textile history (how wool was used in clothing and trade), geography (the Lincolnshire region and its role in British farming) and even global economics (how wool from rare breeds was once traded

Figure 6.4 Bagot Goats explore a working field

across the world). These stories can be embedded into creative tasks such as spinning wool, natural dyeing or writing first-person narratives from the perspective of a shepherd in the 1800s.

Before setting up as a farmer in his own right, Ryan's volunteer work allowed him to work with children and young people who visited the farm, introducing them to animals, and gave him the opportunity to work with placement participants and those with learning disabilities, scaffolding their learning and development with an understanding of why the animals were so important.

His approach to conservation grazing offers a valuable model for others looking to integrate animals into land management practices or considering using animals as a way to support learners to develop a deeper understanding of the natural world, ecology and sustainability. Working on local authority nature reserves and private land, Ryan uses sheep and cattle to manage habitats for ground-nesting birds and native flora, highlighting the creative, community-minded ethos behind his practice.

Results and Impact

What Ryan has created is more than a farm. It's a blueprint for conservation-driven, small-scale agriculture that supports both animals and people. He has proven that it's possible to run a values-led, breed-specific livestock enterprise alongside full-time employment, and that dedication to animal welfare and land stewardship can open doors to leadership, advocacy and meaningful public engagement.

As a practitioner, Ryan embodies the belief that farming can, and should, be built on relationships with animals, with landowners, with neighbours and with heritage.

Lessons Learned

Ryan's case shows that you don't need a big farm or a full-time farming income to make a significant contribution to animal-assisted learning, biodiversity and education. Starting with a few animals, a clear set of values and the determination to work collaboratively can lead to a thriving, resilient and meaningful model of care farming and rare-breed advocacy, which allows animals to stay in their natural habitat and still have a wide impact on learning.

His work also highlights the importance of adaptability, community partnerships and professional development. Ryan's story is a powerful reminder that care farming can be more than a therapeutic offer and can develop into a conservation strategy… and a calling.

> Could a grazing agreement or partnership with a local landowner help you start or expand your animal-assisted project? Are there native or rare breeds that you could introduce to support both animal welfare and land management? Ryan's model shows that a strong ethical foundation, even on a small scale, can have wide-reaching impact.

Josh: Noah's ART

Josh joined Noah's ART at a time when he was feeling quite disconnected. Josh had left formal education and was struggling to find the right fit to continue with learning and work elsewhere, so he felt a bit adrift. He already had a deep love of animals, loads of knowledge about all things lizard and a quiet determination, so it was only natural that he found something transformative in volunteering, along with a sense of belonging and the chance to support others.

Background

Josh first started volunteering at The Pop Inn, which is a community café run by Noah's ART, after he withdrew from formal education. Although he hadn't found success in traditional education systems, Josh was referred to the project by another local college, who were working with him as part of an alternative education provision. Josh brought real expertise in herpetology (reptiles) and quickly became a valued member of the café team, finding himself enjoying spending time in a place where he didn't have to maintain a 'bad boy' image, after being labelled that way by others, and where he felt able to truly show up as himself.

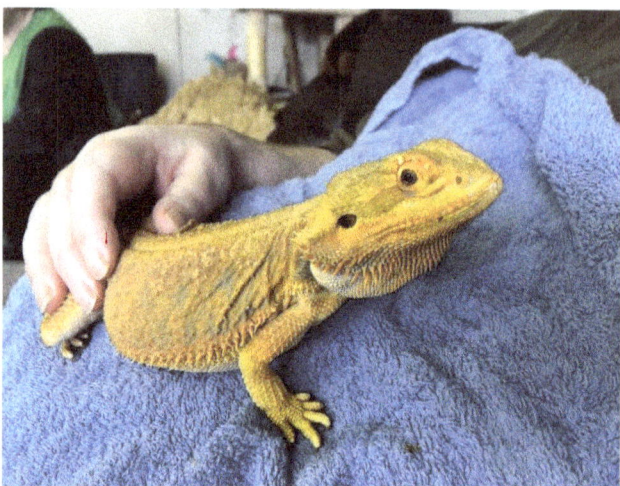

Figure 6.5 One of Josh's reptile friends receiving some affection

Josh describes the Noah's ART environment as one where he doesn't feel judged, where people genuinely care about him and where he can really be himself. 'It's improved my confidence, at the same time as enabling me to help give other people independence and confidence too.'

The shift began in small ways, with Josh receiving positive feedback from others, getting involved in opportunities to share his knowledge, and through gentle encouragement from staff who were trained in therapeutic, animal-assisted approaches.

The Challenge

Josh's situation is not uncommon. Young people who step away from formal education are often seen as disengaged, or as choosing to opt out when, in fact, many of them are searching hard to find the right environment to let them reconnect with learning and development on their own terms.

The people accessing support like this will sometimes struggle to immediately make it work, and Josh did have some initial struggles and disagreements with the team, particularly about his use of language that wasn't appropriate for the environment, where there were often children. Once Josh could picture himself as a role model, he adapted well, his behaviour changed and he was more conscious of his impact, both good and bad.

Noah's ART is an animal-assisted services provider based in Greater Manchester and offer a range of services based around animals, nature and creativity, suitable for all ages. They believe that therapy isn't about 'fixing people' but, instead, think that good therapy is about creating safe spaces where people are empowered to work with animals, form connections and rediscover their value for themselves.

The team's approach is grounded in behavioural activation, a well-researched therapeutic method that encourages action through rewarding experiences. In Josh's case, this meant tapping into his intrinsic motivation, which came from a real love of animals and a deep desire to help.

Approach

Supported Volunteering

After he'd spent a bit of time volunteering in the café at Noah's ART, Josh became a supported volunteer with Pet Connect, which is Noah's ART's dog-assisted befriending scheme. He was mentored on an ongoing basis by coordinators trained in both mindfulness-based practice and animal-assisted therapy, and began visiting clients with a therapy dog after he had completed his initial training.

One such client, 'B', had been experiencing severe anxiety and could no longer walk her own dog, 'S', so Josh and therapy dog Tyler began visiting regularly to support B in regaining confidence.

Figure 6.6 A dog from the dog-assisted befriending scheme, Pet Connect

'Josh and you have enabled me to have the confidence to take S out on my own,' B told the team. 'It's amazing to be a part of.'

And that's one of the tangible and impactful ways that the team are able to create real-world therapeutic benefits for their clients, grounded in oxytocin-rich human-animal interaction, and delivered through a compassionate, structured approach.

Animal-Assisted Therapy, Rooted in Evidence

The approach Josh experienced is underpinned by Noah's ART's therapeutic model. Built on frameworks like behavioural activation, mindfulness and the known benefits of oxytocin in social bonding, the model avoids the clinical lens of pathology and instead focuses on what individuals can do in the present.

Josh's role evolved organically from initial interaction to leadership. He didn't need to articulate goals from day one; instead, the animals acted as the catalyst for building trust, communication and resilience, and Josh was able to consider what his next steps might be at regular touchpoints, as his journey went on.

Confidence, Not Compliance

One of the key therapeutic objectives of Noah's ART. is to encourage beneficiaries to take ownership of their journey. This was central to Josh's experience, and as his confidence

Figure 6.7 Josh's role evolved organically

grew, he began volunteering weekly with pupils from Inscape House School, many of whom had additional needs, and emerged as a role model. That reciprocal sense of trust, empathy and shared purpose is an important part of what makes the experiences at Noah's ART work. They're genuinely reciprocal and collaborative, and the animal, the therapist, the animal handler and, most importantly, the beneficiary all contribute to the process together. It's not driven by the practitioners but is a truly collaborative and unique experience for each person who takes part.

Results and Impact

Josh's journey is a powerful testament to the Noah's ART model in practice. Since joining, Josh has:

- Re-entered formal education via college
- Developed transferable skills and real-world experience
- Found a renewed sense of self-worth and purpose
- Supported isolated adults in the community to regain independence
- Built trusted relationships with children with additional needs

Josh has also become an advocate within the organisation and is currently campaigning (with characteristic determination) for Noah's ART to adopt a resident snake. Staff are yet to be convinced… but with his infectious passion (and a copy of this book!), he may just wear them down.

Lessons Learned

Start with What's Strong, Not What's Wrong

Noah's ART supports individuals who have often felt out of place in traditional systems, but rather than viewing him as someone to be 'fixed', the team saw Josh for who he was: a young person with passion, knowledge and potential. From his first volunteering role at the community café to supporting others through animal-assisted activities, the focus on who Josh was and what he had to offer, rather than what he could 'fix', meant that Josh's journey was built on recognising his strengths and offering opportunities that felt real and meaningful.

Evidence-Informed, Person-Centred Support Works

The model of support at Noah's ART. is deeply person centred, rooted in therapeutic principles such as behavioural activation, mindfulness and oxytocin-rich interaction. These approaches are backed by evidence but delivered in a way that is natural and non-clinical. For Josh, this meant that support didn't feel like therapy. He felt trusted and valued, and benefited from being given space to grow at his own pace.

The Power of Non-Verbal Communication Shouldn't Be Underestimated

A significant part of Josh's growth came through non-verbal communication. The presence of animals allowed Josh to connect without pressure, offering calm companionship and a sense of emotional safety that can often be hard to come by in conversation. Over time, these quiet, powerful interactions helped Josh to build relationships with both animals and people.

Quality Comes from Structure and Care

Underpinning all of this is a structure designed to ensure safety, professionalism and care. Every session is supported by trained staff, robust safeguarding practices and supervision, and there's a focus on adhering to the Society for Companion Animal Studies (SCAS) Code of Practice. Even though the animals that they keep aren't all endorsed by the body, the team have gone out of their way to make sure that they can do the best for the children and animals in their care, scaffolding the external guidance with their own set of policies and procedures for working with exotic animals. While the environment at Noah's ART may appear relaxed and informal, there is a consistent and rigorous commitment to ethical standards, risk assessment and animal welfare that enables everyone, human and animal alike, to thrive.

Small Steps Lead to Big Change

Josh's progress didn't come through sudden transformation, but through a series of small, supported steps. From volunteering at a café to working with clients and pupils with additional needs, Josh's journey is both interesting and impressive, but it wasn't achieved overnight. What stepping stones are you building within your provision?

 Take a moment to reflect on the small steps you could offer. Who in your setting might benefit from a strengths-based approach like Josh did? What passions or interests could you nurture through gentle, supported roles or responsibilities? Write down one small action that you could take this week. Make it something achievable, affirming and based on what that person already loves or does well. Then consider what scaffolding they might need to take the next step, and how you could build that together. Remember – small steps lead to big change.

Cedars School, Gateshead: Animal-Assisted Wellbeing Interventions

Working in a setting where students often face complex barriers to communication, confidence and emotional regulation, the staff team at Cedars School in Gateshead began exploring animal-assisted interventions as a way to support wellbeing. After earlier experiences with chickens and ducks proved logistically challenging during school holidays, the school shifted their focus to a longer-term and more sustainable option – and fell in love with a therapy dog called Poppy!

Background

Poppy supports one-to-one wellbeing walks with the children, settles in classrooms during group lessons and helps create a calm atmosphere that allows children to regulate, feel safe and engage in learning.

Figure 6.8 Poppy is a permanent part of the school family

Poppy is a permanent part of the school family. Living with a staff member outside of school hours and spending her days alongside a higher-level teaching assistant trained in therapeutic work, Poppy's part-time role at school is both structured and instinctive.

The school has found creative ways to incorporate her presence into the curriculum, linking brushing her fur to lessons on personal care, and using dog walks to support PSHE learning around healthy living. This embedding of animal presence into meaningful content helps students to give their learning immediate relevance, and the team's approach helps to build children's empathy as well as practical skills for animal care.

The Challenge

When the idea of introducing a therapy animal was first introduced, some staff were hesitant. Concerns around children's allergies, phobias and hygiene meant that the team began cautiously piloting the approach in one classroom before expanding more widely.

By taking time to build trust among staff and parents, developing clear hygiene routines and putting robust risk assessments in place, including always having Poppy on a lead while she's in school, the staff team were able to alleviate concerns and gradually build a shared understanding of the value animal-assisted work could offer.

The school acknowledges that lots of research is needed and appropriate insurance has been required, and it's been important to remember that Poppy needs care and boundaries too. Poppy's timetable includes structured time in classrooms and break periods for her own wellbeing. Being on a lead can be tiresome, so it helps to proactively plan for Poppy's best interests, including rest time and time to relax and let off steam.

Impact

Poppy's outcomes have been tangible. Staff report improvements in attendance, behaviour and learners' mental health, with Poppy playing a particularly important role in helping children re-engage with school following COVID-19 lockdowns.

Pupils look forward to seeing her, and teachers report that Poppy helps children to feel calm and soothed, and that the children benefit greatly from the unconditional love and tactile play that they receive from Poppy the therapy dog, and that the approach taken helps to build children's empathy, as well as practical skills for animal care.

Lessons Learned

The teacher leading this work encourages others to start small, to research thoroughly and to remember that animal wellbeing must come first. Poppy gets the space that she needs to rest and relax, and her needs are carefully considered in every decision.

While Poppy offers therapeutic support, the school also has a tortoise on site, which is an opportunity for children to learn about caring for others and the routines of animal care.

Some animals, despite seeming low maintenance, aren't sustainable in a school setting due to the constant on-site care they require, even during holidays. In some situations, it might be easier to provide care to animals through one consistent caregiver, rather than through a community effort. Matching an animal's needs to the realities of school life, like Cedars School has, can make all the difference to the success and sustainability of your project.

> How could you build trust within your staff team? Investing time in building trust before your animals arrive can help to create a shared understanding and a smoother, more successful experience for everyone involved. Could you hold an open discussion or staff meeting to hear concerns, questions and suggestions? Might people be more comfortable with an anonymous option like anonymous surveys or sticky-note walls for staff to share worries they may not feel able to raise aloud? How can you help staff to understand the purpose and structure of the animal's time on site? Take some time and consider how you'll provide resources or invite questions in a non-judgemental, supportive space and how you might be able to connect the project to school values like empathy, inclusion or wellbeing.

 Matthew Colley: A School-Based Pracademic

Background

Matthew has been working at a special needs school for over 15 years, where he has created a rich and dynamic learning environment, assisted by a collection of animals that now includes donkeys, emus, goats, sheep, pigs, lizards, snakes, parrots, rabbits and small mammals. What a list!

The Challenge

Matthew's journey into education wasn't a conventional one. He began his career training in animal care before becoming a butcher and, later, took on a role at the school caring for animals after being encouraged to apply by a family member. Although he never planned to teach, his passion for animals, deep care for children and willingness to say 'yes' to new challenges meant that, over time, Matthew was encouraged to take on more responsibility, moving from his role as an animal care assistant to supporting children in the classroom and then adding in teaching BTEC Animal Care and leading hands-on, multi-sensory lessons with learners with a wide range of additional needs.

Figure 6.9 St Luke's is home to a class parrot who can't fly but, instead, roams the classroom on foot

Matthew's classroom is far from traditional. When we interviewed him, we were able to see the bits of tree and natural environment that he's brought in to support the animals (and the children), meaning that the classroom felt calm and welcoming, even via video call! It's also a home to a cheeky blue and gold macaw, some snakes, guinea pigs and reptiles, and when he's not teaching, Matthew's coordinating the care and welfare of the animals across the school. Through his unique role, Matthew has found a way to embed animal-assisted learning into every corner of the school day, offering learners structure, calm and purpose.

In this case study, we're going to focus on the animal provision in Matthew's setting, but if you can't wait to find out more about his career, you'll find more information about that at the top of Chapter 9!

Approach

Practical and Real

Matthew's work is practical, responsive and grounded in lived experience. He's developed a curriculum around caring for animals that prioritises life skills, self-regulation and teamwork, and to hear Matthew talk about it, it's come really naturally to him. While academic outcomes are covered, especially for older students working towards qualifications, the heart of his teaching lies in enabling young people to feel confident, needed and competent.

Cleaning out animal enclosures, preparing food or supporting health checks all become opportunities to practise fine motor skills, follow instructions and build a sense of personal responsibility, as well as to understand about human health and care needs through the lens of caring for animals.

Focus and Empathy

Each year, Matthew reshapes his teaching themes to keep content fresh for mixed-age groups, some of whom might find themselves in his classroom for up to three years in a row. A recent focus has been 'how to care for our pets', including introducing feeding routines, animal health and hygiene, and the need for enrichment, with children working both independently and as teams.

His teaching is underpinned by empathy and humour, and it's obvious when talking to Matthew how he builds strong, trusting relationships with learners. He's kind and warm, and it seems obvious to him that children can sometimes learn about themselves most effectively through shared care for the animals, rather than through a focus on themselves. For some pupils, their connection to a classroom dog like Maple or a quiet moment spent watching a millipede can make all the difference. Children who find it difficult to settle for academic learning sessions can find that having a living, moving insect to focus on becomes the mechanism through which learning can properly begin. When children aren't focusing on 'looking like they're listening', they can actually process and take in what's being said during lessons.

Trauma-Informed Practice

Matthew also brings a trauma-informed lens to his work, allowing children to express themselves safely through interaction with animals, and showing them that feelings, both theirs and others', are valid and visible.

Earlier this year, Matthew taught sessions in the afternoon, after an old sheep died on school grounds. Though visibly upset, Matthew supported children to understand his loss and demonstrated that sadness is sometimes part of our lives. This ability to bring animals into his teaching even at the toughest points allows Matthew to model empathy, care and love for the children he supports, alongside providing ample context for a huge number of opportunities to build real-life skills with his learners.

Challenges

While Matthew's provision is thriving, the work that he does at school isn't without its pressures. The animals' needs are constant and cannot be paused for school holidays, snow days or illness… or even for lessons. Matthew is often the one arriving early, staying late or trekking through the snow to ensure the animals are safe and cared for, and the radio that he keeps on his desk is never entirely silent.

Figure 6.10 St Luke's is also home to donkeys, alpacas, sheep, birds and reptiles, alongside a school dog and numerous small animals

Matthew does have support at school. There's a second member of animal-focused staff, and between them, they provide for the animals as their priority. If there's ever a need to prioritise, the needs of the animals always come top of the list.

Because of this, and the complex nature of building such comprehensive animal provision within a school that supports children with their own diverse needs, Matthew faces the daily challenge of balancing his multiple roles. As a key member of the school's behaviour support team, Matthew is regularly called out to assist with pupils in crisis, which interrupts both his teaching and planning time. And although he is modest about his success, he admits that managing such a large, complex provision with limited time for administration or formal planning can sometimes feel overwhelming.

Matthew is also modest about his abilities in the classroom, talking about 'winging it' with lesson planning when, in truth, Matthew is a skilled practitioner with an uncanny ability to read and scaffold the behaviour and needs of both animals and children, and to build relationships which allow him to 'plan live' using routine animal care activities as a way to embed life-skills learning and academic practice into day-to-day tasks which are enjoyed by both him and his class.

While Matthew's colleagues sometimes borrow his animals to more explicitly 'teach maths', including weights and measures and basic arithmetic, Matthew prefers to take a softer approach, embedding the skills and allowing children to learn through exploration and play, before attaching labels to the learning. This approach contributes to Matthew's reputation

Figure 6.11 Matthew Colley and one of the school's baby Emus who, now fully grown, forms part of the St Luke's provision

as 'safe' and allows him to help children to feel less intimidated by skills building in areas that can otherwise come with negative emotions attached, helping them to learn more easily and feel more confident when learning in other environments.

Studying for additional qualifications in animal-assisted therapy is something that Matthew has wanted to do for a while. We talk more in his career case study, about his approach to learning for himself, but it's another project that has been challenging to fit in around his responsibilities. Matthew is committed to growing his skills and continuing to improve the quality and safety of the provision, which is what's kept him going, but with all of those animals, a full calendar and five children of his own at home, it's easy to find yourself wondering how he ever manages a holiday!

Originally, Matthew had hoped that Maple, his eight-year-old yellow Labrador, who has been at the school since she was eight weeks old, would become a registered therapy dog. But he quickly discovered that therapy registration schemes (like Pets As Therapy) often come with restrictions that don't reflect the kind of informal, child-led, embedded work Maple actually does. He explains that, technically, Maple isn't a therapy dog because of those restrictions, but the reality is that Maple does far more by simply being herself. She sleeps in classrooms, plays on the field and is loved by the children. Her presence is calming, and teachers often request her when classes are unsettled.

Matthew and his colleagues use Maple's presence to help children regulate their behaviour, not through command or reward, but through relationship and shared care. If the class is too loud, the teacher might say, 'Maple's asleep so you'll have to be quiet,' and the children usually respond with empathy and gentleness.

Although Matthew doesn't describe his work as 'therapy' in a clinical sense, what he offers is deeply therapeutic. His animals are used to support regulation, engagement and connection in a child-led, relational way – whether it's a snake calming a child with ADHD, a parrot sitting beside a lesson or a group going out to feed and check on donkeys.

Matthew is clear, however, that animal welfare comes first. Children aren't forced to engage with animals. If they're frightened or disinterested, that's respected. And if an animal needs rest or is unsettled, it's not brought into the classroom. His instincts, which have been honed over years of practice, now with both children and animals, guide what's safe, appropriate and beneficial for both parties.

Results and Impact

Matthew's impact on pupils is deep and long-lasting. Students who previously struggled to remain in class or engage with others have flourished in the environment that he's built. One non-verbal child found focus through handling a millipede, and another discovered confidence through a connection with the class snake. And Maple, the school dog, is often invited into classrooms to help settle unsettled pupils, changing the atmosphere instantly with her presence.

Former pupils frequently return to visit. One learner, told he'd never achieve qualifications, went on to gain a distinction in animal care at college and is now doing well at university. He credits Matthew's lessons, and the opportunity to work with animals, with inspiring and preparing him to pursue that path.

The school itself benefits from the provision in multiple ways. Teachers report improvements in behaviour, attention and classroom climate when animals are present, and the animal-based curriculum provides essential life skills and vocational pathways for learners who may not be suited to purely academic routes... and everyone seems really very happy, which is a huge part of the puzzle!

Lessons Learned

Matthew's journey highlights that passion, perseverance and trust can be just as important as formal training. He's shown that meaningful animal-assisted education doesn't need to start with a grand plan but can, instead, grow organically, shaped by what learners need and what animals make possible. When Matthew started working at the school, there were certainly no plans to raise emus or open an on-site farm, but here we are!

The animals must come first. Their welfare is non-negotiable, and children are taught from day one to respect that. By modelling care, patience and emotional openness, whether through daily routines or in moments of grief when an animal passes away, Matthew helps his learners to develop empathy, their sense of safety and their emotional literacy.

Relationships are central to everything he does, whether it's the trust he's built with school leaders (who will listen to his ideas, no matter how outlandish they might sound at first, and help him to talk them through), the bond between a child and a donkey, or the trust he's built with the flightless macaw, who can be found joining in with lessons from his tall perch. What matters most in Matthew's classroom is that every child feels seen, safe and valued, and that they know, just as the animals do, that they belong here.

What could an animal care curriculum look like in your setting? Matthew's story shows that even in a busy school, animal care can become the heart of meaningful learning. Could you link animal routines to PSHE, science or functional maths? How might animal-assisted tasks support life skills, teamwork or emotional literacy in your classroom?

What do your learners need most, and could animals help provide it? For some children, it's calm. For others, it's context. Could a classroom animal help to reduce anxiety, increase focus or bring joy? Think about which pupils might benefit from non-verbal connection and how you could safely introduce this into your setting.

How can you protect planning time and reduce burnout when animals are involved? Matthew balances teaching with emergency behaviour callouts and animal welfare. If you're thinking of starting a similar project, what support would you need? Could another colleague be trained to share responsibilities? Is there capacity for a volunteer, student or support worker to help with animal care tasks?

Are your senior leaders on board? Strong leadership support has been crucial to Matthew's success. Who in your setting could champion your idea? Could you start by having a conversation about your vision and how animals could support your learners in practical, measurable ways?

What kind of teacher do your pupils think you are? Matthew's pupils don't just remember the lessons; they remember how he made them feel. What might your learners say about you ten years from now? And could an animal-facilitated approach help you create moments that really stay with them?

7

No Room? Don't Worry! Ways to Incorporate Animal Learning Without Animal Care Responsibilities

Now, we know this chapter is about a setting without animals, but to get to where we need to be, first we need to imagine a classroom where the calming presence of a golden retriever helps learners regulate their emotions, or where the curiosity sparked by a tortoise's slow crawl or a snake's slow slithering leads to a rich discussion about biology, patience and empathy. What is it that you're trying to achieve? Remember your objectives?

Selly (2014, p. 173) tells us that animal connection promotes 'authentic experiences that bring children [...] together – including many adaptations if live animals are not permitted'.

Now let's figure out how to achieve all of that without ever needing a dog lead, a litter box or a regular upkeep claim on the school budget.

For many professionals in education or health and social care, the idea of incorporating animals into learning and care provision sounds inspiring but impossible. We'd like to think that we've shown, through case studies, anecdotes and examples, that it's not impossible to have an animal provision anywhere, but something being possible doesn't always make it the right choice.

Limited space, tight timetables, allergies and safeguarding concerns can make traditional animal-assisted education feel out of reach. Or maybe after reading and doing the exercises, you've realised that it's just not the right thing to do for your current cohort of learners. Whatever your reasons for deciding that animal provision isn't for you right now, you don't have to totally miss out on the benefits. What if reduced stress, increased engagement and improved social-emotional learning could be gained without bringing in the actual animals?

This chapter is your guide to doing just that. Here we'll explore creative, practical and proven ways to bring the magic of animal-assisted learning into your learners' lives, without the mess or maintenance.

And if you are still exploring your options for animal provision, you'll find inspiration for activities, imagery and learning that can help to extend and embed your provision, or which might help you to involve your wider school or community.

DOI: 10.4324/9781003649304-7

No Room? Don't Worry! 129

We will begin with ideas for low-resource activities and lesson ideas that capture the power of animal imagery, storytelling, simulations and virtual tools. Later in the chapter, we'll look at what you could do with others, including activities and ideas for working with external animal provision or visiting organisations.

Animal Imagery and Visual Learning

By using photos, illustrations and videos, you can spark curiosity and emotional connection. Remember how we talked about the benefits of observation? Some of those same benefits can come from imagery or video footage.

Unlocking learners' interest in animals doesn't always mean that you have to jump in and buy a class pet, so whether you're searching for alternatives or just looking for warm-up activities to help you to prepare, here are some great ideas for animal provision… without animals!

- **'Animal of the week' visual journal:** With a visual journal, you can display a new animal each week or month, which can form the basis of research projects by your learners. With their journal or sketchbook, learners can independently (or with support) research the animal's habitat, behaviour and adaptations, then spend time creating a visual journal using drawings, facts and personal reflections in a format appropriate to the learners (i.e. research page, lapbook, etc.). Depending on the needs of your learners, this activity could support the development of a wide range of educational, emotional and developmental outcomes, particularly when working with young children or those with SEND. The opportunity to draw, create and personalise the visual journal encourages expressive arts and design, and presenting their journal or writing captions helps children to build language, both verbal and written. The activity is inherently adaptable, allowing learners to use writing, imagery, video or other means to develop and present their research.
- **Emotion mapping with animal faces:** In this activity, you can use expressive animal photos, such as a yawning lion, a curious meerkat or a sleeping pig to explore emotions. Learners spend time considering the images and matching the animal expressions to feelings using emotion labels. Depending on the age and capability of your learners, you might follow this with conversation, or learners could go on to write short stories or diary entries from the animal's perspective. This activity directly supports children in recognising, naming and understanding emotions, which is foundational for self-awareness and regulation. By using animals as the 'mirror', children can explore complex feelings in a way that feels safe and non-threatening. This mirrors Jayne's practice at Goxhill Meadows, where children are asked to interpret animal behaviour as a stepping stone to naming their own emotions. Using an image of a curious meerkat or a yawning lion externalises the feeling, making it easier for children to approach and understand.

130   *Animal-Assisted Learning*

Figure 7.1 Animal emotion cards help children to match feelings to faces

- **Camouflage challenge:** Here you show examples of animal camouflage and ask learners to design their own creatures that could blend into different classroom environments. If you have the space, animals could be created with craft materials and 'hidden' in their camouflage environment, or drawings, paintings or clay models can be used to adapt this activity to your environment. These animal creations can also form the base of an art project where the animal picture is used as a starting point for the learners to create a background in which the animal is hidden. At its core, this activity teaches learners about animal adaptations and survival strategies, specifically camouflage. It introduces the idea that animals have evolved to blend into their surroundings for protection or hunting, and can link directly to curriculum topics in science, such as habitats, classification or life processes.

Simulations and Role-Playing

Learners who aren't able to write or draw or those who prefer to provide verbal feedback might benefit from simulation or role-play exercises in place of journals. Simulations can also help learners to explore concepts and ideas from a new perspective, developing empathy by asking them to, almost literally, put themselves into someone else's shoes. 'Role play simulations support student engagement, critical thinking, and long-term memory retention' (Pettenger et al., 2014).

- **Animal behaviour lab (no animals needed!):** Watch short videos of animal behaviour, such as animals playing or hunting. Learners record observations like scientists or researchers, then hypothesise about the reasons behind the behaviours. While nature documentaries can be good tools for this, they do often come with the barrier of recorded narration, which can influence learners' observations. Look for videos made for pets with woodland animals, live streams from zoo cameras or clips without narration, to help learners to interpret behaviour for themselves.
- **Adopt-a-species campaign:** Ask learners to choose an endangered animal species and help them to create a campaign to raise awareness, including posters, speeches and digital presentations. To increase the impact, this activity can be developed further, with learners assigned points or fake currency to vote for or 'fund' their choice of campaigns, replicating the way that conservation charities work in the real world and helping to prompt conversations about species' role in the ecosystem, how conservation works and issues such as animal habitat destruction. 'Role-playing games are being used to develop collaboration and communication skills, and their educational potential increases when paired with a formal debrief period' (Heinz and Prager, 2019, p. 1).

Virtual Tools and Tech-Based Learning

It's also possible to utilise digital platforms to explore the animal kingdom in immersive ways, and at any scale. 'Digital learning tools enhance personalization, engagement, and flexibility, while promoting collaboration, inclusivity, and continuous professional development' (Srivastava and Srivastav, 2024, p. 6).

- **Virtual zoo tours and live cams:** It's possible to use webcams from zoos and aquariums to observe animals in real time and allow learners to track behaviours and create observation logs. Benefits here include the opportunity to observe different animals across a number of streams, or for the whole class to watch a feed together, which might allow for discussion alongside quiet recording of observations. Live feeds can be found fairly easily online, and many zoos provide access to feeds of enclosures, as well as outdoor spaces, which can allow learners to observe animal behaviours that would usually be inaccessible to humans.
- **AR animal exploration apps:** It's also possible to use augmented reality apps like WWF Together to bring animals into the classroom virtually. These can be helpful for spatial

learning and engagement, and can help bring animal-based learning to life. For children who process information visually or who are developing spatial reasoning skills, AR can help to bring intangible and abstract-feeling ideas into perspective (Hamilton et al., 2021).

In Focus - Real-Life Examples

The following examples offer a view of different activities that have been used with both preschool children and adult learners in a university setting. The studies also offer ideas with and without animals, and using a combination of the two, with visiting animals attending the setting just for the activity.

Postcards from the Hutch - A Preschool Letter-Writing Adventure

As part of an imaginative learning journey, Jenny introduced a magical activity to the preschool setting: an Animal Post Box, specially designed for some very special furry friends - three hamsters and one rabbit.

Alongside the post box, Jenny placed a collection of hamster- and rabbit-themed postcards, which were pre-printed with space for writing and drawing. Children were also given access to a variety of papers and writing materials including pencils, pens, crayons, and markers to help them express themselves in their own unique ways.

Next to the post box, the children found photos of each animal, complete with name cards and descriptions of their personalities, helping them to connect with the animals as individuals with real characters. The children were invited to write or mark-make messages to the animals, asking them questions, telling stories, sharing kind thoughts or even drawing pictures for them. Every message posted into the box received a personal reply from the chosen animal, written on matching rabbit or hamster-themed postcards, making the experience feel even more magical and meaningful.

The excitement and joy this project sparked were wonderful to see. Children eagerly checked for responses, re-read replies and often talked about what the animals had sent to them. They began forming relationships with the animals through the exchange and had the opportunity to display their empathy, curiosity and creativity.

Due to the popularity and enthusiasm around the project, 'the animals' occasionally sent the post box back for another visit, allowing the children to continue their correspondence and keep the imaginative dialogue going.

While fanciful, this project supported early literacy and communication skills through purposeful mark-making and writing, and also encouraged emotional connection, turn-taking and thoughtful questioning. It was a great way to embed for children how meaningful writing can be, even when it is addressed to a rabbit or a hamster!

The Reading Tree – A Storytime Adventure with Animal Friends

'Animals are ideal reading companions… children find reading to an animal less intimidating [which] transforms formerly dreaded reading events into a positive experience' (Wotton House School, 2023).

Jenny's preschool children were invited to take part in a very special reading project by some familiar furry friends, which included three (rather cheeky) hamsters, a curious rabbit and our thoughtful hearing dog friend, Walter, who was a regular visitor to the classroom.

To begin the project, Jenny sent the children a photo of each animal reading their 'favourite' book. These photos were taken in fun and inspiring places (Walter the hearing dog was even spotted enjoying a story in the children's section of the local library!). Along with their photos, the animals each included a special green leaf, and each leaf had the title of the book that the animal was supposed to have read with a few descriptive words to encourage others to give the book a try, describing the books with single words and short descriptions, like 'funny', 'a witch' and 'sparkly pages'.

The leaves were added to a beautiful Reading Tree, which was displayed on our classroom wall. The tree quickly became a central hub of excitement, and next to the tree, Jenny provided a tray full of blank green leaves in a variety of shapes for children and families to take home.

Any child who added a leaf to the tree, reviewing a book that they had read, would receive a bookmark, and they could choose from a dog, rabbit or hamster design.

Every single child chose to take part, and they enjoyed choosing a book to read at home and writing or drawing on their leaf. Jenny really enjoyed watching children proudly adding their leaf to the tree. Some children even sent in photos of themselves reading with their own pets or family animals, which were added to the display and sparked lovely conversations about reading, animals and home life.

As the Reading Tree grew, so did the children's excitement and motivation to read. When we had a copy of a book mentioned on a leaf, we displayed it nearby so friends could look through it too. Choosing a bookmark from the animals became a real, treasured moment for each child.

This project helped to encourage a love of reading and home and school connection, and fostered a sense of shared purpose. The Reading Tree became a real celebration of stories, friendships and the magic that books can bring.

Animal Celebration Day – A Day of Learning and Laughter

Animal Celebration Day was a special event dedicated to celebrating, learning about and caring for animals of all shapes and sizes, which took place in the same preschool setting, at the forest school.

In the days leading up to the event, Jenny introduced a collection point, for the local pet food bank, into the classroom. Children and their families donated a range of items, from fish flakes and hamster treats to dog biscuits, cat toys and even a cosy cat igloo and a dog bed. The growing pile of donations became an easy talking point, which was able to spark thoughtful discussions about animal needs, care and kindness. Some children even chose donations based on animals close to their hearts, proudly explaining who they were donating for.

On the big day itself, the preschool was filled with excitement and activity from the moment the children arrived. All their animal friends, both real and virtual, were included in the celebration, and the classroom welcomed visits from the three alpacas, the chickens and the friendly dog and cat that called the setting home. Even their slithery ball python featured in different parts of the day. Virtually, the hamster friends, rabbit and hearing dog also joined in, with the children creating special celebration hats and flags for the animals to wear remotely. The animals may have been virtual, but their presence felt just as real!

The day included a visit from representatives of the pet food bank charity, who spoke to the children about their work and led a fun, engaging activity that they planned and brought with them. They were touched by the children's generosity and took the donations with thanks, sharing how they would help animals in need.

One of the highlights of the day was the firepit barbecue, where the children helped Jenny to prepare and cook hot dogs. The children were especially excited to cook an extra sausage for their visiting dog friend, who joined us for cuddles, play and a tasty treat (with full permission from their owner, of course!).

Another special moment was when the children gave homemade ice cream, which was animal-safe and prepared the day before, to the alpacas. It was a wonderful act of giving, and the animals certainly seemed to enjoy their cool, creamy treats!

To end this joyful day, children wore their handmade animal hats and waved their flags during a lively Animal Carnival Parade, celebrating all the animals who had been part of our day, near and far.

Animal Celebration Day was not only fun but filled with valuable opportunities for learning, empathy and connection. It reminded us all of the importance of caring for animals and understanding their needs, and it provided the foundation for lots of follow-up activities and links to learning.

Chickens and Creativity – Making Observation Tangible

As part of an ongoing focus on connecting children with the natural world, Jenny's class of preschoolers took part in a fun chicken-themed art project that combined creativity and observation with hands-on animal interaction.

Over several sessions, children created chicken-inspired artworks using a wide variety of art media, including artist canvases, coloured card, textured paper, pencils, pens and various types of paint such as watercolours, poster paint and finger paints. This variety allowed each child to explore different textures and techniques while expressing their unique interpretations of chickens.

In this instance, the children created their artwork while sitting near real chickens. They had the chance to observe the chickens up close, noticing the way they moved, pecked, clucked and fluffed their feathers. The children listened carefully to the chickens' vocalisations, watched as they laid eggs and even had the opportunity to feed and gently stroke them under close supervision.

While this activity took place with chickens that were resident within the school environment, the same activity can be undertaken either by visiting a local city farm or using a web cam feed of chickens or any type of animal that could be linked with a classroom theme or personal interest.

These sensory experiences helped the children develop a deeper understanding and appreciation of the animals, which was beautifully reflected in their artwork. Some children captured the shapes and colours of the chickens with great detail, while others used imaginative and abstract approaches, inspired by the chickens' movements, sounds and interactions.

This project was a celebration of art, but also a nurturing opportunity to build empathy, observation skills and respect for living creatures, which are all essential aspects of early development. The resulting artwork sparked some great conversations about artistic techniques, the living world and animal feelings and behaviour.

 ### Canines, Coffee and Curriculum – A Tail-Wagging Study Support Event for Paediatric Nursing Students

In the final weeks of the academic year, during a time that can feel particularly overwhelming for paediatric nursing students facing their Objective Structured Clinical Examination (OSCE) assessments, dissertation work and two major essay deadlines, a unique and uplifting support opportunity was offered via Canines, Coffee and Curriculum (CCC) sessions.

Running from 10.00 to 12.00, this optional drop-in session was designed to meet students exactly where they were academically, emotionally and socially, and the room was transformed into a multi-zone space where students could revise, reflect and relax in whatever way suited them best.

To support OSCE preparation, a fully resourced practice station was set up, complete with relevant equipment and practice scenarios for students to run through. For the two essay assignments, dedicated stations were created, offering curated reference books, university documents, policies and guidelines. The dissertation station included updated university guides and planning tools, with space to write, organise thoughts or ask questions.

Both Jenny, as the responsible lecturer, and a colleague were present throughout the session for one-to-one questions, guidance and general support, which created a relaxed, yet academic atmosphere where no pressure or expectations were placed on students, just open access to help and resources.

Adding a special animal-assisted layer to the event was the calming and relaxation station, which was a cosy corner filled with beanbags and cushions, and support from two friendly canine companions. The dogs stayed for the full session, happily accepting strokes, snuggles and smiles from students while they were working. Treats and water bowls were provided, and the dogs offered just the right kind of quiet comfort many students needed, as well as helping to encourage calm for the sake of the dogs. They were an undeniable highlight, with many attendees sharing how much joy and calm the animals brought them during a stressful time.

Students were warmly encouraged to bring their own coffee, tea and snacks, and to view the session as a social and supportive revision opportunity with a chance to work alongside peers, talk with lecturers and take a breath before the final push of the term.

The CCC session was incredibly well attended, with almost the entire student group popping in, and many staying for the full-time slot. The feedback was full of appreciation, with students voicing how much the session helped to ease their anxiety, clarify their thinking and boost their confidence.

Based on the feedback and to continue the support, students were informed that on the day of their OSCE exam, a team of volunteer therapy dogs from a national organisation would be in the waiting area. These trained support dogs would be available for stroking, cuddles and calm companionship, with a little 'paw-powered' cheerleading to help soothe nerves and offer reassurance.

 ### On the Farm – Exploring Animal Therapy in Paediatric Care

As part of the university's paediatric nursing curriculum, Jenny's students took part in a unique and enriching experiential learning day at a city farm in London.

This off-campus opportunity offered students the chance to explore the role of animal therapy, including its applications, benefits and therapeutic potential, in supporting children and families in clinical and community settings.

Figure 7.2 Posters, artwork and signage can all help learners to navigate provision safely and learn new things about animals

Figure 7.3 Visits off-site can help learners to contextualise what they've learned and provide opportunities for less formal engagement

To guide and enhance their learning, students were given a custom-designed workbook, created specifically for the day by Jenny. The booklet provided key information on animal-assisted interventions and prompted reflection, observation and active participation throughout the day's activities.

The core focus was to explore how animals and nature can positively impact physical, mental, emotional and social wellbeing, and how these benefits can be applied in paediatric healthcare. To support this learning, the day included a variety of interactive learning stations, each offering a different perspective on therapeutic approaches involving animals:

- **Walter the hearing dog's station:** One of the highlights of the day was a station hosted by Walter, our hearing dog friend, and his owner. This activity focused on the healing power of green spaces and animals, offering students the opportunity to reflect on how outdoor settings enhance therapeutic outcomes. Through a creative arts and crafts session, students contributed to a collaborative art piece, where they decorated a tree on the farm, celebrating the connection between animals, nature and human health (all with the support and permission of the farm manager).
- **Goat yoga (with a twist):** While live goat yoga was not an option at the farm, students explored the concept using toy goats, set up next to the real goat enclosure for a touch of authenticity. This station provided a creative example of how alternative resources can be utilised in therapeutic settings when live animals are unavailable, prompting discussions on adaptability in practice.
- **Play and narrative therapy station:** This space offered a range of animal-themed toys to explore the use of play and narrative therapy in paediatrics, especially for children experiencing trauma or communication difficulties. The station was located beside the horse paddock, showing how live animals and toys can be used together as part of a rich, imaginative therapeutic intervention.
- **Animal therapy posters:** Across the farm, custom posters, designed by Jenny, were displayed near various animal enclosures, sharing facts about the therapeutic benefits of that animal, alongside the British Sign Language (BSL) sign for each. Created and installed with the farm's permission, these posters helped students understand the multi-sensory and inclusive potential of animal interaction.

In addition to structured learning, students had time to engage directly with the farm animals, and were encouraged to bring a ball, frisbee or similar to enjoy the open green spaces. Many made use of this, creating a social atmosphere for movement, play, and peer bonding, while also making it easier to learn in a more relaxed space.

The day was completed with time for animal feeding, animal engagement and a picnic lunch or food purchased from the farm café, giving everyone a chance to enjoy the surroundings and reflect informally on their experiences.

Figure 7.4 Bagot Goats explore a working field

Feedback from students was overwhelmingly positive. They described the day as 'hands-on and memorable', 'a great way to learn outside the lecture theatre' and 'a good mix of fun and focused learning'. One learner reported that this was 'an experience I'd like to do again and even share with my family'.

Many commented on how valuable it was to see, try and experience the ideas in action, and how much they appreciated the opportunity to connect with peers and learning in a new environment.

The farm learning day not only deepened students' understanding of animal therapy in paediatric care, but also modelled creative, accessible and inclusive practice they can carry forward into their future roles as compassionate healthcare professionals.

Could an external visit help to contextualise your learning and add stimulus for longer-term discussions and session plans, which reference the visit and the activities with the animals?

Whether a visit is accessible or you have to stay in the classroom, these ideas and case studies show that you don't need a barn, a budget or a Beagle to bring the transformative power of animal-assisted learning into your classroom or care setting.

Keep imagining, keep adapting and keep looking for ways to bring the heart of animal-assisted learning to life in your practice.

8

FAQs and Troubleshooting

> A quick reference guide full of frequently asked questions, common issues and fast facts which could be used as lesson 'hooks'.

Working with animals in both education and healthcare can be incredibly rewarding, but it also comes, quite rightly, with lots of questions. This FAQ section is here to help you feel confident, informed and ready to create a safe and enriching experience for both the people and animals involved.

General Questions

Question	Answer
Why use animals in education or therapy?	Animals can reduce stress, improve communication, boost motivation, support physical and mental health, open supportive and safe avenues of discussion in counselling (person feels safe and secure when the animal is present), reduce loneliness and isolation, and support emotional regulation.
What types of animals are commonly used?	Dogs, rabbits, guinea pigs, horses, chickens, reptiles and even fish. Each type of animal offers unique benefits and potential outcomes.
Are there risks involved?	Yes/Potentially – for example, allergies, bites, zoonotic diseases or fear of animals. This is why risk assessments for both human and animal participants and hygiene protocols are essential.
Do animals need special training?	Yes. Therapy animals should be temperament-tested and trained for calm, predictable behaviour in busy environments.
What qualifications do staff need?	While the formal qualifications in animal therapy available vary from country to country, staff should at least be trained in animal handling, safeguarding and infection control on a basic level for best possible outcomes. Safe handling, safeguarding and infection control awareness are also best practice for classroom/healthcare provision.

DOI: 10.4324/9781003649304-8

Question	Answer
How do we ensure animal welfare?	Animals must have rest periods, proper housing, regular vet checks and the right to withdraw from interactions. All animal activities need to comply with UK animal laws.
Can animals help with specific conditions?	Yes – animals can support individuals who have been diagnosed as autistic and those with anxiety, PTSD, ADHD and so much more.
What if a student is afraid of animals?	Participation should always be optional. Gradual exposure and alternative activities should be offered and considered best practice.

Best Animals for Different Settings

Animal	Best for	Why
Dogs	Therapy sessions, reading programmes	Highly trainable, emotionally responsive, comforting, well-known animal species, come in a variety of species (colour, size, personalities, etc.). Hypoallergenic breeds can be incorporated into provision.
Guinea pigs	Classroom/therapy pets, sensory regulation	Gentle, low maintenance, good for small group work, small and light to handle, non-fur guinea pig species does exist (skinny pigs).
Rabbits	Emotional support, early years/ care of the elderly, in-patient therapy	Soft, calming, can be handled with care, many different breeds are available offering a variety of choice – small to very large, standard-length hair to long-haired.
Horses (equine therapy)	Physical therapy, trauma recovery, equine counselling	Builds confidence, improves motor skills, improves communication skills both verbal and non-verbal, as well as trust.
Chickens	Outdoor learning, responsibility	Teaches care routines, life cycles, breed selections (vast number of different breeds with unique looks and personalities) and food origins.
Fish	Calming environments, observation	Low interaction, visually soothing, good for mindfulness, good for starting to learn about caring responsibilities.
Reptiles (e.g. geckos)	Science lessons, overcoming fear	Unique, sparks curiosity, teaches respect for differences, used in mental health services, good for elderly or those who struggle to handle and engage with fast-moving animals.

Common Issues and Troubleshooting

Issue	Solution
Allergies	Choose hypoallergenic animals, keep animals in designated areas, inform participants (careers/parents) of the animals going to be engaged with, check known allergies. Where necessary, avoid specific animal use.
Fear or trauma	Offer opt-out options, use photos/videos first, introduce animals gradually, openly discuss the fears and unpick the how/why the fear is experienced, offer alternative animal options.
Animal stress	Monitor behaviour, provide quiet zones, limit interaction time, provide care and comfort –clean/fresh water, food, shade, hideaway, resting place (i.e. blanket, bed, etc.).
Hygiene concerns	Handwashing protocols, regular cleaning of the animal and the animal equipment in line with animal care and breed-specific requirements, no human food near animals, handwashing equipment to be readily available for human participants, where required, as in healthcare settings, disposable pads to be used on laps of patients.
Legal/safeguarding	Ensure insurance for both humans and animals, parental/patient consent, DBS checks for visiting handlers.
Disruption in class	Set clear rules, use animals as rewards, integrate into structured activities, make part of the curriculum offering.

UK Law and Legal Considerations

Key Legislation

Law	Purpose	Relevance to education and healthcare
Animal Welfare Act 2006	Establishes a duty of care to ensure animal welfare	Applies to anyone responsible for animals, including in schools, therapy settings and care homes. Must meet the 'Five Welfare Needs' (see below).
Performing Animals (Regulation) Act 1925	Regulates animals used in exhibitions or performances	If animals are used in demonstrations or shows, handlers must be registered with the local authority (see below for more details).
Pet Animals Act 1951	Regulates the sale of animals as pets	Relevant if animals are rehomed or sold from educational or therapeutic settings.
Animal Boarding Establishments Act 1963	Covers businesses that board animals	Applies if animals are kept on site long-term or overnight as part of a provision.
Riding Establishments Acts 1964 and 1970	Regulates horseriding schools	Essential for equine-assisted therapy or riding programmes. Requires licensing and inspections.

The Five Welfare Needs (Animal Welfare Act 2006)

Anyone responsible for an animal must ensure:

1. A suitable environment – clean, safe, and species-appropriate
2. A suitable diet – adequate food and water
3. Ability to exhibit normal behaviour – space, enrichment and stimulation
4. Housing with or apart from other animals – based on social needs
5. Protection from pain, suffering, injury and disease – regular vet care and humane handling

The Performing Animals (Regulation) Act 1925

Here are some examples of settings and services where this legislation is relevant in relation to education and health care:

Educational Settings

- Animal shows in schools (e.g. mobile zoos or falconry displays)
- Drama or theatre productions involving live animals
- Science demonstrations using trained animals
- Assemblies or enrichment days where animals perform tricks or routines

Health and Therapy Services

- Animal-assisted therapy where animals perform specific tasks or routines (e.g. dogs doing tricks to engage patients)
- Therapeutic performances in care homes or hospitals (e.g. rabbits or dogs performing calming routines)
- Equine-assisted therapy where horses are trained to respond to cues or perform in structured sessions

Key Requirements in the Act

- Registration with the local authority is mandatory.
- Authorities can inspect premises and prohibit performances if cruelty or neglect is suspected.
- Must maintain records of animals and performance types.

What Hooks Could Be Used in Lessons or Therapy to Capture Interest?

- Why do guinea pigs make great listeners?
- What can we learn from a chicken's daily routine?

- What do animals know that we don't?
- If animals could talk, what would they say about us?
- Why do you think people feel calmer around animals?
- Can an animal be your teacher? What might it teach you?

Remember, you are not alone in this. Working with animals in education or care settings can be incredibly rewarding, and it's OK to have questions along the way – it would be weird if you weren't curious! Each setting and service is unique and may require different or extra information, and that's OK. Use this guide as a starting point, and never hesitate to reach out to colleagues, professionals, the local authority or trusted animal welfare groups for further information and support.

Further Resources (UK)

RSPCA (Royal Society for the Prevention of Cruelty to Animals)

- Education hub: Free teaching materials, lesson plans, and activities for schools and youth groups
- Animal welfare advice: Guidance on pet care, wildlife, and farm animals
- Scientific reports and welfare standards: For professionals working with animals in research or structured settings

SCAS (Society for Companion Animal Studies)

- Resources for care professionals: Guidance on including animals in care homes, hospitals and supported housing
- Pet-friendly accommodation checklist: For planning animal-inclusive environments

Blue Cross

- Education talks and lesson plans: Free school visits, online talks and curriculum-linked resources
- Downloadable activities: Worksheets, debates and science lessons for all key stages

9

Finding (or Inventing) Your Own Career Path with Children and Animals

> For those passionate about both education and animal welfare, this chapter is a great roadmap. It explores various career paths, from becoming a farm educator to starting your own care farm. We discuss qualifications, networking and innovative roles that blend these two worlds, providing inspiration and practical advice for forging unique educational careers.

Building and navigating a career around animals might seem like a far-off dream or something that's only possible if you already have years of experience, but an animal-centred career is not only possible, it's entirely achievable from many different starting points, and can be a natural fit for those seeking agile, people-centred careers that prioritise ethics, inclusion and adaptability.

Traditional career ladders used to offer predictability, but those rarely exist anymore, and the idea that you'll get a job after leaving education and stay there forever no longer reflects the winding, diverse journeys that many of us take. The idea of a 'stepping-stone' career rings especially true in the world of animal-assisted education and care farming, where people like Jayne, Matthew, Emzi, Lesley and Josh have each found meaningful work by following their instincts, growing their strengths and being open to new opportunities, even (and especially) when those didn't look like conventional promotions or steps forward.

Jayne began her journey after teaching, Matthew didn't plan to be a teacher at all, and Lesley's therapeutic dog work began after years of working and developing as a speech and language therapist. For each of them, the career they've built emerged not from a mapped-out plan, but from a commitment to their values and a willingness to respond to what was needed. Think about how we've built our business case around being agile and responsive. We started with a rough idea of what we wanted to achieve, shaped it as we went and assessed each opportunity and risk as they surfaced. That's what a successful career plan does too, recognising that learning, growth and impact can come from many directions, and that the path forward doesn't have to be linear.

DOI: 10.4324/9781003649304-9

Whatever your current role, your connection with animals and young people can become a powerful foundation. Start by asking yourself: What do I love about my work now? What kind of moments do I want more of? Who do I want to help, and how can animals support that journey?

Stepping-stone careers allow for exploration, and small steps can lead to big change. Josh's story at Noah's ART began with volunteering in a café and led to supporting others through animal-assisted visits. Emzi's animal management programme started in a prefab and grew into a full-scale, multifaceted provision. You don't need a fully formed plan to begin. You might start by volunteering at a local care farm, developing a single sensory activity with a school pet or inviting a visiting animal provider to collaborate with your setting. These experiences become your stepping stones and help you to build a bridge to whatever comes next, and in the same way that you can use each one to learn what works for your setting and your learners, you can apply the same approach to learning what works for you.

Building your network is an important part of career development, and it's one that's often overlooked in career paths that are less rooted in sales and business. But the truth is that none of the practitioners that we interviewed truly worked alone, even if they're a sole trader with no team. Each story shows the power of collaboration and connection, whether through formal study (like Jayne's EFPT diploma), peer support (as seen in Matthew, Abide and Emzi's teams) or partnerships with schools, local authorities and community organisations. These relationships become both supportive, helping you to know that things will be OK even if they go wrong, and provide a springboard, helping you to reach further.

It's easy to build a network, and you can do this in lots of different ways – sharing your successes online and building social media connections, engaging in peer discussions and meeting new people at specific networking events, or even through your everyday interactions with colleagues and collaborators.

Successful career development is about building your own version of success. For you, that might include undertaking formal qualifications, or it might involve deepening your practical knowledge, growing your confidence through mentoring or shaping your current role to reflect your passions. Matthew's story, in particular, shows that credibility and impact aren't tied to titles. His impact comes from the authenticity, trust and love that he brings to his work.

Matthew Colley

At the time of our interview, Matthew had worked at the same special needs school for 15 years. His background is practical and hands-on after he originally studied animal care at college, where he was told his practical skills were great, but his academic work wasn't the best, and he had a relatively negative experience of academic learning. After leaving college, he worked on a farm and then trained as a butcher, spending eight years in the trade before deciding to try something new. Animals were always his first love, and when a family member told him about a job opportunity that would allow him to put his animal-based learning and skills back into daily practice, he jumped at the chance.

Matthew never set out to be a teacher. In fact, his transition into education was accidental rather than planned. Matthew's mother-in-law told him about a role looking after animals at a school – the same school he works at today. He applied, got the job and has never looked back.

Matthew's career is a great example of staying agile when career planning. After finding his first job, he's remained open to new learning and new experiences, and has, incrementally, developed skills, language and relationships which scaffold the career that he has now.

When making deliveries for the farm, he stopped to help the local butcher on a busy day and found himself an unexpected job offer and a chance to pursue something totally new, before leaving to start work as an animal care assistant and being coaxed into teaching and developing skills and passion as an educator. While Matthew maintains that he doesn't want to become a qualified teacher, he's currently training as a qualified animal therapist, to help him to develop his practice in other ways.

Animals Came First

For Matthew, animals have always been at the heart of everything. At school, he started out as the animal care manager, taking over the role from a former caretaker who had introduced some animals to the site.

At the time, there were only a few animals on site, including some rabbits and reptiles, which were kept in unsuitable housing by a caretaker with good intentions but little knowledge.

Matthew quickly began to transform the space. With a growing reputation and the trust of senior leaders, he took in rehomed and rescued animals, designed new enclosures and expanded the school's provision into something more like a smallholding. The donkeys, emus, pigs, goats, parrots and reptiles now living both inside and outdoors at the school are a testament to his commitment and his ability to bring people with him.

It wasn't long after starting to work at the school and interact with the children before Mathew began taking part in some lessons. From the beginning, he noticed something powerful in the way that the animals were able to calm children who were unsettled, non-verbal or otherwise struggling. Observing children quietly watching a millipede while taking in their lesson, stroking a guinea pig to find calm or laughing at a goat's antics when dealing with something difficult at home, Matthew could see the connection, calm and confidence that animals had the ability to bring to children's school day. He says that there was 'just something there'.

It's clear that Matthew's priority is always the animals. He puts their needs first, even before his own workload. As he says, 'If I didn't have the animals, I would have no lessons.' And it's that deep sense of responsibility that shapes everything he does, but the care he has for the children that he now supports alongside his animal provision shines whenever he talks about his teaching.

That's the other reason that the animals come first. Prioritising the children's needs might seem more obvious, but co-regulating with classroom companions means focusing on their needs first. As well as providing a calmer, safer and more rewarding environment for the children, focusing on the animals' needs allows Matthew to develop his relationship with his learners by demonstrating love, compassion and care for a shared interest. When the children can see that Matthew cares about the animals, they can more easily recognise the care he has for them and for their classmates. It's a win-win.

'I Don't Want to Be a Teacher'

Despite the fact that Matthew now teaches a full timetable, including the BTEC in Animal Care, he is quick to point out that teaching was never his plan. 'I don't want to be a teacher,' he says, 'but it's what I do.' It's a role he has grown into, shaped by his relationship with the students and his belief in the value of what he teaches.

Working specifically with children who have SEND, Matthew centres all of his learning around the animals in his care. His classroom doesn't look like anyone else's. There's often a parrot wandering across the floor or climbing up to his ceiling perch, and lessons can include anything from checking the temperature of reptile enclosures to hand-feeding goats or preparing feed for pigs. But it works, and students learn, grow and thrive under his care.

There's a little pressure at home, sometimes, for Matthew to pursue a PGCE, so that he can be recognised as a fully qualified teacher, but he's happy doing what he does. As in his career so far, Matthew isn't chasing more money or a more impressive title but seeking to enjoy every day that he goes to work.

What Matthew loves most isn't standing at the front of a classroom and teaching theory, which is part of the reason he's keen to retain his role as it is, rather than formalise his teaching status and accrue further responsibilities. What lights him up is being with the animals and seeing what those animals bring out in the children he supports. When a non-verbal child makes eye contact with a snake or a young person with anxiety finds calm stroking a guinea pig, he sees those moments as magic. He's passionate about the idea that animal care teaches life skills – teamwork, problem-solving, empathy, and emotional regulation – and knows that those skills are important in every area of life, including laying the groundwork for children to be better academic learners and more equipped for vocational study.

Finding (or Inventing) Your Own Career Path 149

Matthew's role has grown and changed constantly, and he's adapted with it. From writing new risk assessments so that he can take in homeless animals to supporting children experiencing crisis, no two days are the same when working with both children and animal (what's that saying again?). The only constant is that Matthew says 'yes' to ideas, to animals in need of homes and to children who want to learn differently.

He's clear that none of this would be possible without trust. His school leaders understand the value of what he does, and he's developed a way of navigating risk that allows him to move quickly and safely. Sometimes he'll float an idea, such as taking in a rehomed animal, and talk it through informally before completing full paperwork. That flexibility means that provision can evolve organically, without bureaucracy getting in the way of animal care, and that Matthew feels safe bringing his ideas to the decision maker before they're fully formed, allowing him to gather feedback early and use it to build a stronger case when he does make his request official.

Although Matthew still says he's 'not very academic', he's currently completing a qualification to become an Animal-Assisted Therapy Practitioner. He's honest about the challenges, which include finding time, managing distractions and staying focused, but determined to keep learning. He's also a sponge for practical information, spending his free time watching animal documentaries and absorbing knowledge wherever he can. There's absolutely no denying that Matthew is following his passion. His belief in the work keeps him going, and he's proud of how far he's come.

Because he naturally gravitates towards more hands-on, immediate tasks rather than written coursework, Matthew is candid about how hard it can be to sit down and concentrate on study, but he's committed to completing it, not necessarily to change his role, but to deepen his understanding and add weight to what he already does.

Matthew sees qualifications as helpful, but not the heart of the work. His bond with Maple and the role of animals across the school aren't built on certificates or checklists – they're built on trust, consistency and care.

Matthew's career path is unconventional but inspiring. He didn't start with a plan, but by following what he loved, he has built a career that blends purpose, passion and play. He knows who he is, what he cares about and what makes a difference for his pupils.

Matthew is the embodiment of that common phrase 'Find a job you love and you'll never work a day in your life'. Although his work is constant and demanding, and requires him to bring his whole self to work every day, he glows with happiness when talking about it all. He's working hard, but seems a little surprised that people think he's doing great things, because he's having a really good time doing them.

Matthew isn't looking for a promotion or a pay rise. He doesn't want recognition as a 'real teacher' by completing a PGCE. He cares much more about doing the work that matters, every day, in a way that's true to who he is.

And for those wondering whether it's possible to build a life around animals without becoming a vet or zookeeper, Matthew's story is pretty solid proof that with passion, patience and persistence, it's possible to create a role that didn't exist before, even if you're not trying to, and to shape your own definition of success.

What does a 'dream career' look like for you?

Matthew didn't follow a set path – he followed what he loved and built his work around it. What parts of your current role do you love most? Could you build something new around those, even if it starts small?

Matthew's role didn't exist until he created it. Could you explore how to gently shape your current job into something that includes animal interaction, perhaps through a pilot, enrichment activity or lunchtime group?

Where will your first 'yes' come from?

Your agile, animal-assisted career might grow slowly and organically or suddenly, in leaps and bounds. What matters most is that it's shaped by your values, sustained by your curiosity and focused on the connections between people and animals. Abide's career with animals in education started very differently to Matthew's. Rather than being led by animals to learning, Abide's teaching career took him somewhere totally different, before bringing him back to his roots and allowing him to develop a participatory project where animals form a core part of his educational offer.

Abide Zenenga

Abide's story begins in rural Zimbabwe, where he walked 7 km each day to school and tended to his father's cattle in the evenings. Starting with a deep love of learning, he trained as a secondary school teacher and found early success supporting deaf learners in a pioneering inclusive education programme as an English teacher.

That passion, and his talent, earned him a place on a prestigious scholarship programme to study in the UK. Although, due to the political climate at the time, his decision to move to Britain was somewhat contentious at home, meaning that he had to choose between the opportunity to study in the UK and his job, Abide decided to take up his place on the scholarship and went on to complete a master's degree and PhD with a focus on participatory action research.

Obviously, we know from our case study in Chapter 6 that Abide came back to education later, founding Riverside Education with his business partner. Although there's not immediately a clear link between Abide's research career and his home in teaching, the 'golden thread' that holds his career together becomes obvious when he talks about his school.

Throughout it all, he's kept one guiding question at the heart of his work: 'What do the people who are affected by this want and need?'

From Research to Riverside

When Abide's son was born with Down syndrome and was later diagnosed as autistic, he found a new understanding of disability and society. He wanted to build a school where children like his son could thrive. A chance meeting with a British businessman, now his closest friend and business partner, provided the opportunity.

Together, they created Riverside. Abide took on the headship, not through an application process, but because the role needed to exist. 'I appointed myself,' he says, 'and I felt guilty about that for years.' But when the school received an Outstanding rating from Ofsted, he allowed himself a moment of pride and reassurance.

Although he's the driving force behind the school's provision, Abide insists on giving credit to the whole team: 'Parents, staff, students, my business partner… Riverside isn't me. It's all of us.'

This is true. Because of the collaborative and needs-focused nature of the way that Riverside is structured, everyone's opinion matters, and learners, colleagues, parents and partners all have input into how best to take each project forward. It belongs to everyone.

As discussed in the case study about Riverside's animal provision, the dream of working in such a collaborative atmosphere, with a community of passionate and knowledgeable stakeholders, also comes with its own challenges, and sometimes this can lead to disagreements. Here too, Abide leads with humility and humour, rather than taking unilateral decisions as Head. In conflict resolution, he asks his team to question: 'Is this resolution good for either of the parties involved in the disagreement, or good for you?' If the answer is the latter, he encourages reconsideration. His background in research comes in handy again here and helps him gather input from every corner of the community, even when that means managing disagreement.

His decisions around animal provision, for example, weren't driven by personal passion (Abide describes himself as 'a plant person'). Instead, he saw how important animals were to the children, and he adjusted his plans for the curriculum and provision accordingly. He models care, even for animals he doesn't naturally connect with, because he knows it helps the students feel safe and seen.

From the outside, Riverside looks like a seamless success story, but the path has been full of conflict, compromise and courage. Abide has faced personal criticism, unexpected public scrutiny and emotional burnout. He's been accused of not caring enough about animals… and of caring too much.

Urban-based animal education projects, such as city farms, school farms and community farms, do often face more public criticism than their rural counterparts, and practitioners introducing animals to unfamiliar settings might need to be prepared for this additional feedback, and the form in which it arrives. In urban environments, where people may have little regular exposure to farm animals or land-based food production, there can be an understandable gap in knowledge about what constitutes good animal welfare, what appropriate habitats look like and how care routines are managed responsibly. For example, the sight of a muddy paddock, a pig lying in a sun-warmed patch of soil or a sheared sheep might alarm someone who hasn't grown up with those realities, mistaking natural or seasonal variations in animal condition or environment for neglect. Without lived experience, it's easy for concerned bystanders to misinterpret the normal signs of a well-managed and enriched farm environment.

The best response is often pre-emptive: embedding educational opportunities for the wider community, being transparent about care routines and holding yourself to clear ethical and welfare standards.

Through it all, Abide has kept his focus on the children. If they're happy, engaged and learning, then the work is worth it. He's also learned when to ignore the noise. 'People will always have opinions,' he says. 'But the animals are well, the children are happy, and we're doing the right thing.'

Abide's journey proves that leadership doesn't have to be linear. He didn't chase headship. It became necessary for him to achieve his goals. He didn't plan to build a farm school, but the children needed one. He stays agile, principled and willing to learn.

One of the most powerful lessons in Abide's story is his willingness to accept support when it was offered. Riverside School wouldn't exist in its current form without the trust, generosity and belief of his business partner, who not only invested financially but allowed Abide the freedom to lead with his values. Despite facing doubts from both their communities, their partnership has grown from mutual respect. Accepting help didn't mean giving up control or compromising the vision. Instead, it meant bringing it to life with someone who believed in it too. For anyone building something from the ground up, this is a reminder that you don't have to do it alone and that the right people, when trusted, can make all the difference.

The imposter syndrome hasn't gone away completely. 'Sometimes I think – shouldn't someone else be doing this?' But the joy of seeing a child bond with a chicken or a withdrawn learner thrive through animal care reminds him that he's exactly where he needs to be.

 Who are the people who believe in your idea, even if they don't fully understand it yet? Think about who you could bring into your circle of support. Is there someone who could offer time, skills, space or funding, if you were willing to ask?

Jenny's own journey speaks a little to the idea of working things out as you go and not taking no for an answer. You might not experience the same level of support that Abide found to help bring your idea to life, but it's clear that regardless of the backing you have to begin with, working to overcome challenges and continually defend and sell your idea will be a key element if you want to succeed.

Jenny Phillips

Jenny has never followed the path laid out in front of her. Instead, she's built her own. Jenny's path is one that blends early years education, nursing, forest school and animal therapy, and, somehow, feels like a comprehensive and straightforward path.

It's a true 'stepping-stone' career, with each opportunity allowing Jenny to develop, grow and find her bearings before taking another step towards her next goal.

Jenny's professional life began with a childcare qualification and progressed into nursing. She trained as a paediatric and neonatal intensive care nurse, and later taught child health at university. But it was her enduring love of animals and her belief in their ability to support human development that led her to question the boundaries between sectors. Could animals belong not only in hospitals and homes, but in nurseries and classrooms?

That question set her on a journey of study, practice and experimentation that hasn't stopped since.

What questions are guiding your career? Could you write down one question you're currently holding about your work, your learners, or your next step? What might happen if you followed it?

Since the age of 16, Jenny has never gone a year without formal study. Her qualifications span childcare, SEND, forest school, animal therapy, leadership and health. She holds multiple degrees, is currently undertaking a second master's and has also worked on doctoral research in animals and health.

But Jenny is quick to protest that she's not the 'academic type.' She's dyslexic, a visual learner and a doer by nature. 'I'm hands-on. My brain doesn't work in a box... I think it works in another galaxy,' she jokes. Her study habits include spider diagrams, colour-coded notes and staying up until 2 am with animal therapy texts, and she's driven by a brain full of questions and an unrelenting drive to answer the one constant question: 'What if...?'

As a 'pracademic', Jenny scaffolds practice with research and links all of her learning back to real actions. Jenny's advice to others? Passion comes first. If you care about something enough, you'll find a way to learn what you need to know. And if you don't like the standard route, find another way in.

Do you need a formal qualification to get started? Could you try a short course, webinar, book club or podcast first? Learning doesn't have to be linear – or lonely. Even social media has opportunities to learn. Follow accounts which showcase animal provision, learning tools or lesson plans that you can learn from as you scroll.

Jenny didn't choose between early years or animals, and she's gone out of her way to build a life that allowed her to have both. That's meant saying yes to the unusual, the impractical and the improbable, and letting go of the need to be certain. Her decisions have meant that her days at school involve cuddling alpacas, walking snakes and advocating for micro pigs in classrooms... alongside working with health boards and schools to write risk assessments no one had written before.

Jenny credits her confidence to being determined and prepared. When people say no, Jenny doesn't give up. She researches, argues and reframes until she finds a route forward. 'No is where I start,' she says. 'No is a conversation, not an answer.'

And that's partly where the idea for this book came from!

Who could help you shape your 'yes'? If you're facing resistance, find someone to play devil's advocate and practise making your case. Prepare the answers to the questions before they're asked.

There are no boundaries unless you put them there. Jenny has proved that early years, special needs, animal therapy and health care don't have to exist in silos. Not only is it possible to make it work, but it can work incredibly well! If your passion bridges disciplines, even if they might seem unconventional partners, follow it.

Don't wait for a job to exist. You can create your own. Jenny didn't follow the standard pathway to management or leadership. Instead, she designed roles that reflected what mattered most to her, and then found settings that were willing to give her the freedom to grow. The job advert that she applied to made no mention of animals, but Jenny knew what she wanted to achieve when she started in her post... and how she wanted to get there.

Say no to 'no'. Whether it's a reluctant senior leader, a cautious parent or your own inner critic, Jenny reminds us that 'no' is not the end of the conversation. It's the beginning of your next good idea. Use objections to add new dimensions to your idea, iron out wrinkles and shape your offer. No is just a starting point.

Mix and match what you love. Just because no one else has combined your passions doesn't mean it's impossible. Jenny's path has been powered by imagination, grit and the firm belief that 'if it hasn't been tried, it can't be disproved'.

 What are your ingredients? Write down three things you love. What might it look like to build a career or a project that holds all of them? Could you take the first step this year?

So, while it might seem 'woolly', there's no single right way to build a career that includes animals and education – only the way that works for you. Whether you're starting from a classroom, a care background, a health service or a muddy field, you already have valuable tools available to you. Your passion, your curiosity and your willingness to say 'what if' are enough to get started. You can build everything else as you go and, whether you're looking to complete one successful project and move on or develop a career rooted in animals and education, the stories here remind us that changing careers can be creative, responsive and joyful, and that changing your career doesn't always involve changing jobs.

You don't need to have all the answers to take your first step, just a clear sense of what matters to you and the courage to keep going, even if the route feels unconventional. Surround yourself with people who believe in your ideas, build your knowledge in the way that suits you best, and remember: every small step counts. You don't need a farm or a PhD to make a difference – just a little space, a lot of heart and the belief that learning and care can go hand in hand.

BIBLIOGRAPHY

Agile Business Consortium (2025) Membership-based working groups and learning resources. [online] Available at: www.agilebusiness.org [Accessed 23 June 2025].
American Humane Society (2014) Canines and Childhood Cancer: Pilot Study Report. [online] Available at: www.americanhumane.org/app/uploads/2016/08/cccnovpilotstudyapril2014.pdf [Accessed 27 September 2025].
AP News (2018) Goat yoga brings a different feel to fitness in Cyprus. [online] Available at: https://apnews.com/article/lifestyle-health-yoga-85d80572ac354668b1061f2590773277 [Accessed 27 September 2025].
Bandura, A. (1977) *Social Learning Theory*. Englewood Cliffs, NJ: Prentice Hall.
Berbel, M. and Praetorius, R.T. (2023) The therapeutic power of goat yoga: Exploring outcomes and experiences. *Social Work in Mental Health*, 21(2), 105-122.
Birkett, P. (2023) The healing power of animals. [online] Available at: www.sirpeterbirkett.com/the-healing-power-of-animals [Accessed 21 June 2025].
Blanchard, A. (2015) *Therapeutic Beekeeping: Nature Connection and Mental Health*. London: Greenfield Press.
Bowlby, J. (1969) *Attachment and Loss: Vol. 1. Attachment*. New York: Basic Books.
Brelsford, V.L., Meints, K., Gee, N.R. and Pfeffer, K. (2017) Animal-assisted interventions in the classroom: A systematic review. *International Journal of Environmental Research and Public Health*, 14(7), 669. https://doi.org/10.3390/ijerph14070669.
Carehome.co.uk (2024) Enhancing well-being: Pet therapy flourishes across our homes. [online] Available at: www.carehome.co.uk/news/article.cfm/id/1709106/enhancing-well-being-pet-therapy-flourishes-across-our-homes (Accessed: 27 September 2025).
Chandler, C.K. (2012) *Animal-Assisted Therapy in Counselling*. 2nd edn. New York: Routledge.
Choudhury, P. (2025) Exploring the significance of animal pictures. [online] Available at: https://myzootopia.com/articles/animal-pictures-education-conservation-social-media [Accessed 5 July 2025].
Cole, K.M., Gawlinski, A., Steers, N. And Kotlerman, J. (2007) Animal-assisted therapy in patients hospitalized with heart failure. *American Journal of Critical Care*, 16(6), 575-585. https://doi.org/10.4037/ajcc2007.16.6.575.
Costa, A. and Kallick, B. (2000) *Habits of Mind, Vols. I, II, III and IV*. Alexandria, VA: ASCD.
DeKruyf, L. (2008) An introduction to narrative therapy. Faculty Publications – Graduate School of Counselling, George Fox University. https://digitalcommons.georgefox.edu/gsc/15 [Accessed 8 October 2025].
Fanson, K. (2022) *Effective Storytelling to Engage Learners*. London: Learning Press.
Fine, A.H. (ed.) (2010) *Handbook on Animal-Assisted Therapy: Theoretical Foundations and Guidelines for Practice*. 3rd edn. San Diego, CA: Elsevier Academic Press.
Fine, A.H. (ed.) (2019) *Handbook on Animal-Assisted Therapy: Foundations and Guidelines for Animal-Assisted Interventions*. 5th edn. London: Academic Press.
Ford Sori, C. and Ciastko Hughes, J. (2014) Animal-assisted play therapy: An interview with Rise Vanfleet. *The Family Journal*, 22 (3), 350-356. https://doi.org/10.1177/1066480714534394.

Gee, N.R., Fine, A.H. and McCardle, P. (eds) (2017) *How Animals Help Students Learn: Research and Practice for Educators and Mental-Health Professionals*. Abingdon: Routledge.

Glamour UK (2017) I did yoga with a goat on my back and it was surprisingly zen. [online] *Glamour*. Available at www.glamour.com/story/i-did-yoga-with-a-goat-on-my-back-and-it-was-surprisingly-zen [Accessed 27 September 2025].

Hamilton, D., McKechnie, J. and Edgerton, E. (2021) Immersive virtual reality as a pedagogical tool: A literature review. *Education and Information Technologies*, 26(3), 2931-2950. https://doi.org/10.1007/s40692-020-00169-2.

Isaacs, B. (no date) Why sensory experiences are the foundations of early learning: Learning and development, Teach Early Years. Available at: www.teachearlyyears.com/learning-and-development/view/children-learn-through-their-senses [Accessed: 27 September 2025].

Kolb, D.A. (1984) *Experiential Learning: Experience as the Source of Learning and Development*. Englewood Cliffs, NJ: Prentice-Hall.

Laird, D. (1985) *Approaches to Training and Development*. Reading, MA: Addison Wesley Publishing Co.

Lewis, H. and Grigg, R. (2020) *Tails from the Classroom: Learning and Teaching Through Animal-Assisted Interventions*. London: UCL Press.

Martin, F. and Farnum, J. (2002) Animal-assisted therapy for children with pervasive developmental disorders. *Western Journal of Nursing Research*, 24(6), 657-670. https://doi.org/10.1177/019394502320555403.

McCardle, P., McCune, S., Griffin, J.A. and Maholmes, V. (2011) *How Animals Affect Us: Examining the Influence of Human-Animal Interaction on Child Development and Human Health*. Washington, DC: American Psychological Association.

McCune, S., Griffin, J.A., Maholmes, V. and Hurley, K. (2014) Animal-assisted interventions in mental health: Opportunities and challenges. *American Psychologist*, 69(6), 541-552.

McGee, M., Townsend, M. and Findling, R.L. (2018) *The Role of Companion Animals in the Treatment of Mental Disorders*. New York: Springer.

McGee, M., Townsend, J. and Findling, R.L. (eds) (2022) *The Role of Companion Animals in the Treatment of Mental Disorders: A Comprehensive Review of the Evidence*. Cham: Springer.

Morris, K. and Lewis, H. (2017) Farm animal-assisted interventions: Empathy and motor skills development. *Journal of Therapeutic Practices*, 5(1), 20-30.

National Education Union, State of Education: Teacher stress and wellbeing | national education union (2025) National Education Union. Available at: https://neu.org.uk/press-releases/state-education-teacher-stress-and-wellbeing [Accessed: 27 September 2025].

NCFE (2020) S1E11 - Dawn learns about the Neuroscience of Early Childhood and Education with Mine Conkbayir. POD-CACHE [podcast], 9 January. Interview by Dawn Newman. Available at: https://podcache.podbean.com/e/s1e11 [Accessed: 10 August 2025].

NCFE (2020) S2E06 - We all have our own Brain Story - Dawn learns about children's brain development with Dr Elizabeth Rapa and Dr Louise Dalton. POD-CACHE [podcast], 10 June. Interview by Dawn Newman. Available at: https://podcache.podbean.com/e/s2e06 [Accessed: 10 August 2025].

NCFE (2020) S2E04 - Dawn talks to Dr Shawna Lee and Andrew Freeman about child development, parenting and coregulation. POD-CACHE [podcast], 11 May. Interview by Dawn Newman. Available at: https://podcache.podbean.com/e/s2e04 [Accessed: 10 August 2025].

O'Haire, M.E. and Rodriguez, K.E. (2018) Preliminary efficacy of service dogs as a complementary treatment for posttraumatic stress disorder in military members and veterans. *Journal of Consulting and Clinical Psychology*, 86(2), 179-188. https://doi.org/10.1037/ccp0000267.

Omar, S. (2025) *The Power of Storytelling in Education*. Oxford: Insight Academic Publishing.

Pettenger, M.E., West, D.M. and Young, R. (2014) Assessing the impact of role play simulations on learning in international relations. *International Studies Perspectives*, 15(4), 491-508. www.jstor.org/stable/44631220.

Pichot, T. (2011) *Animal-Assisted Brief Therapy: A Solution-Focused Approach*. New York: Routledge.

Pichot, T. (2016) *Animal-Assisted Brief Therapy*. New York: Routledge.

PMI (Project Management Institute) (2021) *A Guide to the Project Management Body of Knowledge (PMBOK® Guide)*. 7th ed. Newtown Square, PA: Project Management Institute.

Prager, R.H.P. (2019) Exploring the use of role-playing games in education. *The MT Review*, 2. https://mtrj.library.utoronto.ca/index.php/mtrj/article/view/29606/25764 [Accessed 8 October 2025].

Scrum.org (n.d.) The Scrum Guide™. [online] Available at: https://scrumguides.org [Accessed 31 July 2025].

Selby, A. and Wright, L. (2014) *Connecting Animals and Children in Early Childhood*. London: Routledge.

Selly, P.B. (2014) *Connecting Animals and Children in Early Childhood*. St. Paul, MN: Redleaf Press.

Srivastava, M. and Srivastav, R. (2024) Digital learning tools enhancing educational outcomes: A review of current trends. *British Journal of Educational Technology*, 55(1), 22–38.

Stanley-Hermanns, M. and Miller, J. (2002) Animal-assisted therapy: Therapeutic interventions. *Nursing Clinics of North America*, 37(1), 121–131.

Swansea University (2023) Animal-assisted education: Research and projects. IsSel [online] Available at: www.swansea.ac.uk/social-sciences/research/cenprac/research-projects/animal-assisted-education/#recent-activities=is-expanded&relevant-publications=is-expanded [Accessed 27 September 2025].

Tedeschi, R.G. and Jenkins, S.R. (2019) *Transforming Trauma: The Role of Animals in Recovery*. New York: Routledge.

Tedeschi, P. and Jenkins, M.A. (2019) *Transforming Trauma: Resilience and healing Through Our Connections with Animals*. West Lafayette, IN: Purdue University Press.

Ulrich, R.S. (1984) View through a window may influence recovery from surgery. *Science*, 224(4647), 420–421. https://doi.org/10.1126/science.6143402.

University of Nebraska Medical Center. (2022) Research shows therapy dogs give Alzheimer's patients, Newsroom. Available at: www.unmc.edu/newsroom/1999/10/25/research-shows-therapy-dogs-give-alzheimers-patients [Accessed 27 September 2025].

Vanfleet, R. and Faa-Thompson, T. (2017) *Animal Assisted Play Therapy*. Sarasota, FL: Professional Resource Press.

Vanfleet, R. and Faa-Thompson, T. (2018) *Animal Assisted Play Therapy*. New York: Routledge.

VanFleet, R. and Faa-Thompson, T. (2010) A case for using animal assisted play therapy. *British Journal of Play Therapy*, 6, 4–18. https://risevanfleet.com/wp-content/uploads/2023/01/Case4AAPT.BJPTWinter10_4-18.pdf.

Wesenberg, S., Mueller, C., Nestmann, F. and Holthoff-Detto, V. (2019) Effects of an animal-assisted intervention on social behaviour, emotions, and behavioural and psychological symptoms in nursing home residents with dementia. *Psychogeriatrics: The Official Journal of the Japanese Psychogeriatric Society*, 19(3), 219–227. https://doi.org/10.1111/psyg.12385.

Winslade, J. and Monk, G. (1999) Narrative Counseling in Schools: Powerful and Brief. Thousand Oaks, CA: Corwin Press.

Wikipedia (2025) Animal-assisted therapy. Available at: https://en.wikipedia.org/wiki/Animal-assisted_therapy [Accessed 21 June 2025].

Wikipedia (2025) Classroom pet. Available at: https://en.wikipedia.org/wiki/Classroom_pet [Accessed 21 June 2025].

Wikipedia (2025) Equine-assisted therapy on autistic people. Available at: https://en.wikipedia.org/wiki/Equine-assisted_therapy_on_autistic_people [Accessed 21 June 2025].

Wilson, E.O. (1984) *Biophilia*. Cambridge, MA: Harvard University Press.

Wotton House School (2023) Animal-assisted learning. Available at: www.wottonhouseschool.co.uk/animal-assisted-education [Accessed 27 September 2025].

INDEX

Note: Page numbers in *italics* refer to Figures.

academic and cognitive skills 9-11; *see also individual subjects*
adopt-a-species campaign 131
allergies 34, *35*, 40, 41, 50, 67, 73, 96, 120, 128, 140, 142; hypoallergenic animals 106, 141, 142
alpacas 21, 104, 105-106, 107, 134, 154
anchor, sensory 11-12
Animal Boarding Establishments Act 1963 142
Animal Celebration Day 134
Animal Education Centre: Emzi Mills-Frater 55, 88-93, 145, 146
Animal Welfare Act 2006 142, 143
Animal Welfare (Licensing of Activities Involving Animals) (England) Regulations 2018 101
animal-centred way of working 98
annual animal day 48
apps, augmented reality 131-132
Aristotle 5
assemblies 47
attachment theory 28
attention deficit hyperactivity disorder (ADHD) 15, 126, 141
augmented reality apps 131-132
autism 17, 99, 141
autonomy 20, 44, 75, 105

badge, kindness keeper 48
beetles 35
behaviour and wellbeing 12
behavioural activation 115, 116, 117
benefits, holistic 4
biodiversity 108, 110, 111, 113
birds 106; ground-nesting 112; migrating 109; parrots 121, 122, 126, 127, 148
Blue Cross 144
body language 11, 65, 97, 105, 106-107

boundaries, personal 44
box breathing 47
breathwork 17, 43-44, 47
burnout 62; checklist for avoiding 69
business case 70-71; benefits 74-76, 91; building 74-82; conclusion and call to action 82; costs and financial plan 71-72, 79-81; executive summary 74; how to use objections 72-73; objectives and benefits 74-76; options considered 76-79; parental approval 41; principles of 71-72; project plan 81-82; risk assessment *see separate entry*; scoring your 72; template 74
businesses, local 90
butterfly hug 47

calendar reminders 57
calming techniques 47, 50; breathwork 17, 43-44, 47; *see also* grounding
camouflage challenge 130
care of animals 39, 45-46, 121, 142; Animal Celebration Day 134; enrichment 32, 45-46, 51, 52, 89, 92, 123, 143; five welfare needs: Animal Welfare Act 2006 143; growth charts and feed logs 47; mission creep 56; Northern Animal Assisted Therapies and Activities (NAATA) 94, 95, 97, 98; risk assessment 61-62, 63, 64, 65; Riverside Education 84, 85, 86, 87; routines 44-45, 52, 105, 121, 123, 124; school-based pracademic: Matthew Colley 122-124, 126, 127, 148; temperamental rehomed cat 105; therapy dog in school 120; welfare log 69; wider school community 47
care farming 39, 113, 145, 146
career path 145-155

case studies 83; Animal Education Centre: Emzi Mills-Frater 55, 88-93, 145, 146; Cedars School, Gateshead 119-121; Colley, Matthew 121-127, 145, 146-150; Goxhill Meadows Hearts and Minds 99-103, 129; Josh: Noah's ART 113-118, 145, 146; Northern Animal Assisted Therapies and Activities (NAATA) 93-98; Perry, Ryan 107-113; Phillips, Jenny 104-107, 153-155; Riverside Education 83-87, 150-152
caterpillar-to-butterfly cycles 38
cats 104, 105, 106, 107, 134
cattle see cows
Cedars School, Gateshead 119-121
charities 80, 90, 134, 144
charter, animal 48
checklists: avoiding burnout 69; environment and practical set-up 51-52; intention and planning 49-50; preparing children and staff 50-51; risks 67; routine building and integration 52; setting up for safety 68; whole-school culture and celebration 53-54
chickens 24, 34, 36, 37, 52, 87, 93, 94, 104, 106, 119, 134, 140; best for and why 141; chick hatching 38; cockerels 110; and creativity 135; small-scale conservation farming 107, 110
child-led interaction 105
chinchillas 24
choice of animal(s) 31-35, 49-50; best for and why 141
citizenship 109
city farms 39, 135, 136-139, 152
co-regulation 4, 8, 11-12, 15, 17, 18, 42, 55, 61, 68, 76, 100, 103; animals' needs 49, 148; checklist: preparing children 50-51; first few weeks 43-44; whole-school culture 47, 48
cognitive and academic skills 9-11; see also individual subjects
collaborative: classroom culture 75; role-playing games 131; and unique experience 117
colleagues 41, 47, 51, 120, 121; potential conflict with see risk assessment
Colley, Matthew 145, 146-150; school-based pracademic 121-127
communication 9, 11, 17, 75, 95, 96, 97, 99; barriers 8, 119; gap 27; non-verbal 11, 118; play 27-28; role-playing games 131; see also body language
community interest company (CIC) 93
connection 87, 96, 128; bridge to 27-28
conservation farming: Ryan Perry 107-113
cortisol 15, 23
costs 109; and financial plan 71-72, 79-81

cows 19, 34, 35; small-scale conservation farming 107, 109, 110
cross-curricular integration 12-13, 43; see also individual subjects
culture and history 111

dementia care practice 23-24
design 36, 40; hybrid models 39-40; permanent provision 39, 77, 78-79; provider visits school 37-38, 77; time-bound projects 38-39; visit animals in own environment 38, 78
Dewey, J. 6
dogs 32, 66, 103, 104, 123, 134; Animal Education Centre 90, 91; best for and why 141; child-led interaction 105; dementia patients and therapy 23-24; different breeds of 34; mobility stability aids 22; motivation to exercise 22; NAATA: therapy 93, 94, 95-96, 97; Noah's ART's dog-assisted befriending scheme 115-116; paediatric nursing students 135-136; school-based dog: Maple 123, 125-126; therapy dog: Cedars School (Gateshead) 119-121; therapy registration schemes 125
donkeys 121, 126, 127
dyeing, natural 112

E. coli 65
economics 111-112
education, health and care plans (EHCPs) 101
emotion mapping with animal faces 129
emotional development 8-9, 23; regulating emotions 15-17
empathy 9, 17, 44, 87, 103, 105, 117, 127; Animal Celebration Day 134; cats 106; chickens 34, 106, 135; dogs 97, 120, 126; focus and 123; meaningful interaction 20; neurobiology 15; preschool letter-writing 132; shared responsibility 75; simulations and role-playing 131
empowering learners 84-85
emus 121
endings 39, 123, 127; Goxhill Meadows Hearts and Minds 102, 103
endorphins 25
enrichment 32, 45-46, 51, 52, 89, 92, 123, 143
environment 45-46, 86, 89; enrichment 32, 45-46, 51, 52, 89, 92, 123, 143; and practical set-up checklist 51-52; risk assessment 65; setting up for safety checklist 68
epi-pens 41

ethical tensions 56
external provider visits school 37-38, 77; *see also* Forrester, Lesley

farm animals 34-35, 38, *39*; city farms *39*, 135, 136-139, 152; mobile farm 37; pupil placements at care farm 39; purchase of farm 83-87; rare and heritage/specialist/native breeds 39, 86-87, 107-113; *see also* chickens; cows; goat(s); pigs; sheep
farming, care 39, 113, 145, 146
farming without a farm 107-109; costs 109; educational partnerships 108-109; small-scale conservation farming: Ryan Perry 107-113; storage for feed and bedding 109
fears or phobias 41, 106-107, 126, 141, 142
ferrets 24, 32
fish 24, 140, 141
fleas and mites 66
food bank, pet 134
food education 34, 38
food security 111
forest school context 104, 105, 107, 134, 153
Forrester, Lesley 145; Northern Animal Assisted Therapies and Activities (NAATA) 93-98
frequently asked questions (FAQs) 140-141
funding 47; costs and 71-72, 79-81; flexible 71-72, 79

Gardner, H. 7
genetics 87, 111
geography 38, 109, 111
gerbils 89
goals *see* objective(s)
goat(s) *19*, 34, 41, 73, 87, 90, 103, 121, *139*, 148; pygmy 35; small-scale conservation farming 107, 110, 111; yoga 21, 138
Goxhill Meadows Hearts and Minds 99-103, 129
grants 80
grounding 103, 106; *see also* calming techniques
guinea pigs 31-32, 122, 148; best for and why 141

Haigh, Jayne 145, 146; Goxhill Meadows Hearts and Minds 99-103, 129
handwashing 65, 68, 90, 93, 142
hens *see* chickens
history and culture 111
holiday care planning 47, 54
holistic benefits 4
hooks to capture interest 143-144
horses 32, 35, 40, 100, 102, 103; best for and why 141; Human and Equine Interaction Register (HEIR) 101; Riding Establishments Acts 1964 and 1970 142; small-scale conservation farming 111
Horses in Therapy and Education International (HETI) 101
Human and Equine Interaction Register (HEIR) 101
hybrid models 39-40

imagery and visual learning 129-130
immune conditions 41
in-breeding 110
insects 24, 35, 109, 123; stick 38
insurance 120, 142

Josh: Noah's ART 113-118, 145, 146
journals 47, 52, 57; 'animal of the week' visual 129

know your animals 105

language arts 12, 43, 53, 112, 132-133; Reading Tree 133; Riverside Education 84
learning blocks 21
learning disabilities 112
legislation 101, 142-143
licences 35, 101, 142
lizards 121
local authority 80, 102; inspection 101; nature reserves 108, 112; registration with 143

macaw 122, 127
matching child to animal 106, 107
mathematics 9, 12, 43, 53, 124; Northern Animal Assisted Therapies and Activities (NAATA) 95, 97; Riverside Education 84, 85
memory books 102, 103
metaphor and mirroring 100
millipedes 123, 126
Mills-Frater, Emzi 55, 88-93, 145, 146
mindfulness 17, 115, 116, 117, 141
mission creep 56-57
mites and fleas 66
Montessori, M. 6
motor skills 5, 11, 12, 17, 22, 34, 96, 105, 123
music 43

narrative therapy 26-27, 138
native flora/wildflowers 109, 112
nature-based learning 5-7
network: career development and building 146; support 47, 51, 69, 146
neurobiology 15
neurodiversity 97, 99
neurological complications, patients with 22
neuroplasticity 22

newsletters 47, 48
Noah's ART: Josh 113-118, 145, 146
non-verbal/speaking children 8, 64, 99, 126, 147, 148
Northern Animal Assisted Therapies and Activities (NAATA) 93-98

objective(s) 29-31, 42, 46, 55; and Key Results (OKRs) 31, 49, 55, 57, 74-76; mission creep 56-57; scope creep 56-57
observation-based early sessions 43
one-to-one sessions 43
oxytocin 15, 116, 117

paediatric nursing students: animal therapy in paediatric care 136-139; canines, coffee and curriculum 135-136
parent(s) 40-42, 96, 103, 120; update 47
parrots 121, 126, 148; macaw 122, 127
patience 17, 127
Performing Animals (Regulation) Act 1925 142, 143
permission, parental 41
Perry, Ryan 107-113
pervasive developmental disorders (PDD) 9
Pet Animals Act 1951 142
Phillips, Jenny 104-107, 153-155
phobias or fears 41, 106-107, 126, 141, 142
physical benefits 11-12; coordination 11, 22-23; grooming animals 22-23; motor skills 5, 11, 12, 17, 22, 34, 96, 105, 123; muscle control 22; pressure manipulation 22-23
physical education 12-13
physiotherapy 22
pigs 121, 148, 152; micro 106; small-scale conservation farming 107, 109, 110, 111
planning: case studies 84-85, 86, 87; checklist: intention and 49-50; choice of animal(s) 31-35, 49-50, 141; design see separate entry; objective(s) see separate entry; parental involvement 40-41; project plan 81-82; succession and holiday care 47, 54; see also business case; preparation; risk assessment; routines; whole-school culture
planning permission 85
play 19-21, 27-28
post-traumatic stress disorder (PTSD) 32, 141
posters, animal therapy 138
poultry see chickens
pregnancies: infections in sheep and human 66
preparation 40; checklists 50-54; children 42, 50-51; colleagues 41, 51; parents 40-42

preschool setting: Animal Celebration Day 134; chickens and creativity 135; letter-writing 132-133; Reading Tree 133
proprioception 96
psychological power of animals 4, 9, 15-28; regulating emotions 15-17
psychological safety 4, 9, 14, 55

questionnaires 40, 96
questions to capture interest 143-144

rabbits 7, 32, 43, 65, 66, 85, 106, 121; best for and why 141
Rare Breed Survival Trust 109, 110-111
rare and heritage/specialist/native breeds 39, 86-87; conservation and education 110-111; history and culture 111; small-scale conservation farming: Ryan Perry 107-113
rats 18, 86
Reading Tree 133
registration 35; Performing Animals (Regulation) Act 1925 143; therapy dogs 125
rehomed animals 89, 105
reptiles 24, 34, 84, 90, 105-106, 122, 140, 147, 148; best for and why 141
responsibility 44; caring for animals 17, 20, 75, 87, 105, 123
retreat zones for animals 51, 65, 68
Riding Establishments Acts 1964 and 1970 142
risk assessment 21, 44, 58, 81, 118, 120, 140, 149; adding controls 63; Animal Education Centre 89, 90; bought or rescued animals 89; checklists 67-69; feedback 66; hazards 62-63; research 66; review and update 66, 81; risk levels 64-65; starting 59-62; teacher wellbeing 60-64, 69; templates 65
Riverside Education 83-87, 150-152
role-playing 131
roundworm 66
Rousseau, J.-J. 6
routines 105, 121, 123, 124; building 44-45, 52
RSPCA (Royal Society for the Prevention of Cruelty to Animals) 144
rules: adult present 44; reasons for 44

safe spaces 42-44, 51, 68, 115
SCAS (Society for Companion Animal Studies) 144; Code of Practice 118
schizophrenia and skunks 25
science 12, 34, 35, 38, 53, 109, 130; Northern Animal Assisted Therapies

and Activities (NAATA) 97; Riverside Education 84
scope creep 56-57
self-esteem 9, 21, 25, 32, 75
self-regulation 4, 17, 20, 27, 75, 92, 95, 97, 122
sensitivities 41, 106
sensory: benefits 11-12, 14, 23; connection 4-5, 55; learning 105-106; processing difficulties 11, 106
sheep 7, 34, 41, 65, 66, 87, 99, 121, 123, 152; small-scale conservation farming 107, 109, 110, 111-112
simulations and role-playing 131
skunks and schizophrenia 25
small steps lead to big change: Noah's ART 113-118
snails 13, 35
snakes 35, 86, 104, 105-106, 107, 121, 122, 126, 134, 148
social development 8-9, 87, 105
social lubricant effect 28
social media 146
Society for Companion Animal Studies (SCAS) 144; Code of Practice 118
special educational needs and disabilities (SEND) 17-19, 34, 80, 84, 93, 96, 104, 105, 129; Matthew Colley: school-based pracademic 121-127, 148
Steiner, R. 6
strategic relationships: Animal Education Centre 90
strengths-based approach 117
substance dependence syndrome treatment 24-25
succession planning 47, 54
surveys 40

tasks: rotation of 45; visual timetables or lanyards 45; *see also* routines
tech-based learning 131-132

theoretical foundations 5-7, 55
therapy, animal 1-2; behavioural activation 115, 116, 117; emotional and physical 21-22; in paediatric care 136-139; Performing Animals (Regulation) Act 1925 143
to-do list 57
tortoises 24, 121
training 47, 51, 86, 140; dogs 95, 97, 98; staff training bank 48
trauma-informed practice 51, 99, 104, 123
troubleshooting 142

United States 106

videos 129, 131
virtual tools and tech-based learning 131-132
visit animals in own environment 38, 78; *see also* farm animals; Goxhill Meadows Hearts and Minds
visits to schools by external providers 37-38, 77; *see also* Northern Animal Assisted Therapies and Activities (NAATA)
volunteers: network of 47; Noah's ART 113-118; parents 41; supported volunteering 115-117

wall display 47
webcams 131, 135
welfare log 69
wellbeing 12; *see also* risk assessment
whole-school culture/approach 46-48, 53-54; Riverside Education 83-87
wildflowers/native flora 109, 112
wool, spinning 112
WWF Together 131

Zenenga, Abide 84-85, 86, 146, 150-153
zoo cameras, live streams from 131
zoonotic diseases 66, 68

For Product Safety Concerns and Information please contact our EU
representative GPSR@taylorandfrancis.com
Taylor & Francis Verlag GmbH, Kaufingerstraße 24, 80331 München, Germany

www.ingramcontent.com/pod-product-compliance
Lightning Source LLC
Chambersburg PA
CBHW081946230426
43669CB00019B/2941